P.A.T.H.
Prospect. Assess. Test. Harvest.
by Brian Olson & Robin Joy Olson

Copyright © 2025 Brian Olson and Robin Joy Olson
Published by White Dog Inc.
ISBN: 979-8-9991520-0-8
All rights reserved. No part of this publication may be reproduced, distributed, or transmitted in any form or by any means, including photocopying, recording, or other electronic or mechanical methods without the prior written permission for the copyright holders, except in the case of brief quotations embodied in critical reviews, scholarly articles, or other permitted uses under copyright law.

For permission requests, please visit: OfficialOlsons.com

For our grandsons, William and Michael

This is for you and for the generations that follow. Everything we've built, we've built with you in mind. May your dreams be vast, your path be bright, and your courage unshakable.

Acknowledgments

We want to express our deep gratitude to the coaching clients, workshop attendees, and content consumers who have invited us into their stories. Your commitment, your questions, your breakthroughs have shaped this book more than you know.

Each of you has helped us refine the P.A.T.H. framework by living it out in the real world. Thank you for letting us be part of your journey. It's been an honor to walk beside you as you've built businesses, reclaimed time, and found your own version of success.

We're also especially grateful to Jim Cockrum, whose mentorship, generosity, and steady belief in others have opened doors for us and countless others. Thank you for inviting us to grow and contribute inside the incredible community you've built. This book wouldn't exist without the space you made for us.

This book belongs to all of you, too.

With heartfelt thanks,
Brian Olson & Robin Joy Olson

Table of Contents

Foreword	i
About This Book	v
About the Authors	vii
Preface	ix
Introduction: Your Path to Amazon FBA Success	3
Chapter 1: Why Amazon FBA?	12
Chapter 2: Keepa the Story Straight	24
Chapter 3: The Prospect Phase	34
Chapter 4: The Assessment Phase	74
Chapter 5: The Test Phase	112
Chapter 6: The Harvest Phase	142
Chapter 7: The Future's So Bright	170
Chapter 8: Pulling it All Together	180
EPILOGUE	202
INDEX	206

Foreword

When I first met Brian and Robin Joy Olson, it was obvious that they were a dynamic, determined team with their eyes fixed on building a beautiful business online. That's exactly what they've done! They also had an even stronger drive to help others succeed. Many of the thousands of business building warriors in our community have been directly touched by Brian and Robin's mentorship, and we are just getting started! Over the years, I've watched them grow into two of the most inspiring and giving leaders and teachers in our community. I couldn't be more thrilled to see them pour some of their wisdom, energy and heart into the book you are now reading. They've become beacons of what's possible in the exciting world of e-commerce and Amazon selling.

The opportunities ahead of us in e-commerce are indeed limitless, and with the help that Brian and Robin Joy offer you in the following pages I envision a new wave of sellers unlocking the potential of the Amazon platform in ways that are both innovative, scalable and sustainable. At the core of their approach is the Replens model. It's a system our community created and has refined over years of real-world testing. It's a strategy that stands out for its stability in a marketplace that can otherwise sometimes feel like a roller coaster. While trends come and go, the Replens model has offered a steady foundation for thousands of sellers as a way to build a business with minimal downside risks and unlimited upside potential.

Brian and Robin have mastered the art of teaching sellers how to start small, test smart, and scale with confidence while keeping their investment and exposure minimal. Your success in e-commerce is not about chasing the next big gamble; it's more likely a simple matter of finding some of the millions of boring, easily sourced replenishable opportunities on Amazon that deliver consistent results.

So, as you dive into what Brian and Robin have to share, know this: you're in the hands of two extraordinary leaders who live what they teach. They're not just coaches—they're practitioners who've built their own success on Amazon and now dedicate themselves to helping you do the same. The future is bright, the model is solid, the risk is low, and the community is here to cheer you on. With Brian and Robin by your side, you're not just starting a business—you're joining a movement. Let's go build something amazing together!

Jim Cockrum, SilentJim.com

About This Book

This book wasn't born in a boardroom. It was built in the messy middle — between sourcing and coaching calls, in late-night strategy sessions, and through real conversations with real sellers trying to figure it all out.

We wrote this for the people who are tired of feeling overwhelmed, tired of bouncing from one tactic to another, tired of wondering if they're just not cut out for this.

We wrote it for the people who are cut out for this but just need a system that works.

The P.A.T.H. framework is that system. It's not a magic formula, but it is a clear, repeatable way to build something that lasts. It's the process we wish we'd had when we started. And it's the process we've now shared with thousands of third-party sellers who have turned chaos into clarity, and confusion into consistent wins.

Whether you're launching your first test or stabilizing a six or seven-figure business, we hope this book becomes more than just a manual. We hope it becomes a trusted companion on your journey, one that speaks to your goals and your humanity.

About the Authors

Brian and Robin Joy Olson are a husband and wife team of entrepreneurs, coaches, and creators of the P.A.T.H. framework. Together, they blend strategy, heart, and high-energy coaching to help third-party sellers build Amazon businesses that align with their numbers, their lives, and their future goals.

Robin Joy is a creative powerhouse, equal parts artisan and coach, with a passion for turning chaos into momentum. She holds a master's degree in business leadership and brings deep experience in product development, data analysis, and organizational growth. After surviving a hemorrhagic stroke, she pivoted into eCommerce alongside Brian, helping to shape the mindset and systems that now guide hundreds of sellers toward clarity and confidence. Outside of business, she's an avid knitter who finds joy and renewal in the rhythm of fiber and needles.

Brian is the builder, a systems thinker with an MBA, a lifelong entrepreneurial streak, and a deep sense of loyalty to the people he serves. He launched his Amazon business as a side hustle in 2019 and transformed it into a sustainable, scalable operation that powers their shared mission. Known for making complex ideas simple, Brian is committed to walking alongside sellers as they learn, grow, and succeed. He specializes in helping people take focused, confident action without getting overwhelmed.

They live in Colorado, close to their son, daughter-in-law, and two grandsons, surrounded by creative projects and plenty of strong coffee. This is their debut book, a practical and heartfelt guide drawn from years of real, messy, and meaningful work helping people create businesses that genuinely enrich their lives.

Preface

When we started our Amazon FBA journey in 2018, we had no idea how profoundly it would change our lives. Like many of you, we began by consuming endless podcast episodes and YouTube videos, searching for the "secret" to Amazon success. In April 2019, we made our first significant investment in our future - hiring an Amazon FBA coach. By year's end, we had grown our business to over $20,000 in monthly sales and hired our first contractor who lived in another part of the country and did shopping at regional stores for us.

The years since have brought a whirlwind of growth, challenges, and learning experiences. We scaled past $50,000 monthly in 2020, hired contractors and virtual assistants, experimented with more regional shoppers, and navigated the complexities of prep and accounting services. We've tried more tools, calculators, and subscriptions than we can count. Through it all - the successes and failures, the laughter and tears - we've maintained a "boutique" style e-commerce business, generating mid-six figures in annual revenue and consistent six-figure profits.

Our journey has included everything from a failed brand launch (which we later turned around) to speaking at major events, hosting a weekly podcast, and creating educational content that has helped hundreds of sellers find their own

path to success. We've been both students and teachers, learning valuable lessons that only experience can provide.

But here's what stands out after all these years: while tools, services, and strategies come and go, the fundamentals remain unchanged. You'll notice this book doesn't focus on a lot of specific tools, service recommendations, or constantly changing Amazon policies. Instead, we concentrate on what we call the "sources of truth" - Amazon listings and Keepa (historical) data. These fundamentals have remained constant throughout our journey, providing reliable guidance regardless of market conditions or policy changes.

This book distills our years of experience, hundreds of coaching sessions, and millions in sales into a framework that focuses on these unchanging principles. We've seen too many sellers get distracted by shiny objects and temporary shortcuts, only to struggle when those strategies inevitably become obsolete. The P.A.T.H. framework we share here is built on foundational principles that have proven their value through market shifts, policy changes, and economic fluctuations. It is because of this that we spend as much time as we do learning about Keepa in "Chapter 2: Keepa the Story Straight".

Our goal isn't to show you how to make a quick profit or find the "perfect" product. Instead, we want to give you something far more valuable - the confidence that comes from understanding and applying fundamental principles that stand the test of time. Once you master these basics, you'll be equipped to evaluate any new tool, strategy, or opportunity that comes your way.

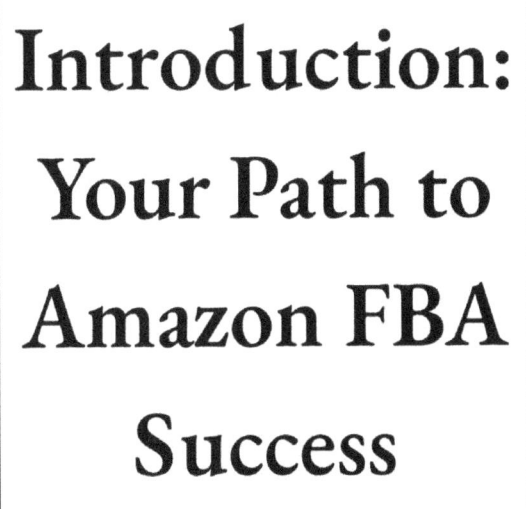

Introduction: Your Path to Amazon FBA Success

Introduction: Your Path to Amazon FBA Success

Brian: I remember the moment clearly. I was sitting at my desk, staring at the screen, paralyzed by the endless sea of Amazon listings. Every product felt like a coin toss. One side said "opportunity." The other said "expensive mistake."

If you've felt like this, you're not alone. For the last four and a half years we've worked with hundreds of sellers who started exactly where you are now, asking the same questions: "How do I know if I'm choosing the right product? What if I invest my savings into inventory that doesn't sell? Am I missing something crucial that could make or break my business?"

The Power of Systematic Success

These are exactly the right questions to ask. But here's what we've learned after years in the Amazon FBA business: success isn't about having all the answers on day one. It's about having a reliable system to find those answers, step by step. That's exactly why we developed the P.A.T.H. framework -

to provide that systematic approach to building a successful Amazon FBA business.

For years, we've taught these principles through our intensive 2-Day "Path to 100 ASINs Accelerator Workshop." While this live, interactive experience remains the fastest way to master these concepts, we've decided to share these valuable insights with a broader audience through this book.

Understanding the P.A.T.H. Framework

Think of P.A.T.H. as your roadmap to building a sustainable, predictable, scalable Amazon FBA business. Through our own experiences as sellers and our work coaching hundreds of entrepreneurs, we've distilled the complex process of building an Amazon business into four critical stages:

1. Prospect Phase: In this initial stage you'll learn to identify VIABLE ASINs using our **Pre-Flight Inspection** process. This systematic evaluation method helps you quickly assess any Amazon listing to determine its potential. You'll also master **Bridging the Gap**, our established approach to connecting with reliable, authorized sources for your inventory.

Introduction: Your Path to Amazon FBA Success

2. *Assessment Phase*: Here, we apply our proprietary **3-Step Check** to evaluate market potential. You'll learn to identify TESTABLE ASINs - listings that show clear evidence that you can recover your investment even if you don't make a profit. This stage removes the guesswork from your decision-making process.

3. *Test Phase*: Through a structured **4-Week Testing** process, you'll gather real-world data about your products without risking your entire investment. This stage helps you identify REPLENISHABLE ASINs - listings where you can confidently reinvest because they meet your minimum profit requirements.

4. *Harvest Phase*: This final stage is where you transform successful tests into reliable, replenishing profits. Here, your Amazon business evolves from a collection of products into a predictable, sustainable, and scalable operation.

P.A.T.H. - Prospect. Assess. Test. Harvest

Introduction: Your Path to Amazon FBA Success

Real Success Stories

The power of this framework is best illustrated through the success stories of sellers who've implemented it. One of our workshop participants arrived completely paralyzed by analysis, spending countless hours researching products but never feeling confident enough to take action. By applying the Prospect and Assess stages of P.A.T.H., he quickly learned to identify promising opportunities. Within mere months he was generating over $10,000 in monthly sales through systematically tested and verified listings.

Another success story comes from someone who attended multiple workshop events and approached Amazon FBA as a way to supplement her retirement income. Initially concerned about making costly mistakes, she used the Test and Harvest stages to build a catalog of profitable ASINs that now provides steady, reliable income. Most importantly, she achieved this without experiencing the stress, uncertainty and loss of capital that plagues so many new sellers.

Your Journey to Freedom

These stories aren't outliers. They're examples of what happens when everyday sellers follow a proven system.

P.A.T.H. - Prospect. Assess. Test. Harvest

P.A.T.H. isn't just about finding profitable products. It's about creating freedom. The freedom to work from anywhere. The freedom to protect your time, your energy, and your dreams.

That's what we want for you. Not just revenue, but resilience. Not just answers, but clarity. Not just a business, but a future you can actually enjoy.

Your Path Forward

Building an Amazon FBA business doesn't have to feel like a game of chance. You don't need to rely on luck or guess your way to success. What you need is a clear path forward, a systematic approach that takes the guesswork out of every decision you make.

That's what this book offers. Whether you're just starting your Amazon journey or looking to bring more intention and scalability to your existing business, you'll find the guidance you need in these pages.

Are you ready to transform your Amazon FBA journey from guesswork to groundwork? Let's begin your path to sustainable success!

P.A.T.H. - Prospect. Assess. Test. Harvest

Chapter 1: Why Amazon FBA?

Your Path to E-commerce Success

" I was working two jobs and barely making ends meet when I first heard about selling on Amazon," a retail professional turned successful Amazon seller tells me, laughing as she remembers her initial doubts. "My friend kept talking about FBA—Fulfillment by Amazon—but all I could think was 'Yeah right, like I could sell anything on Amazon." Today, this Workshop graduate and former skeptic runs a six-figure Amazon business from her laptop, working fewer hours than she did at either of her previous jobs.

Let's begin where she started—understanding what makes Amazon FBA uniquely positioned for your success, especially if you're new to e-commerce.

The Amazon Advantage: A Dominant E-commerce Force

Consider these staggering numbers:

- In 2023, Amazon had over 300 million active customers worldwide and more than 200 million Prime members in the U.S. alone.

Chapter 1: Why Amazon FBA?

- The average Prime member spends $1,400 per year on Amazon purchases. 85% of Prime members shop on Amazon at least once every two weeks.

- Amazon captures over 50% of all e-commerce sales in America. For every $100 spent online in the U.S., more than $50 flows through Amazon.

- While traditional retail grows at 2-3% annually, e-commerce consistently grows at 15-20% per year, with Amazon driving much of this growth.

- These numbers tell a powerful story: Amazon isn't just another marketplace; it's THE marketplace where customers go first to buy online. By selling on Amazon, we tap into this massive, growing customer base that prioritizes convenience and trusts Amazon's platform.

P.A.T.H. - Prospect. Assess. Test. Harvest

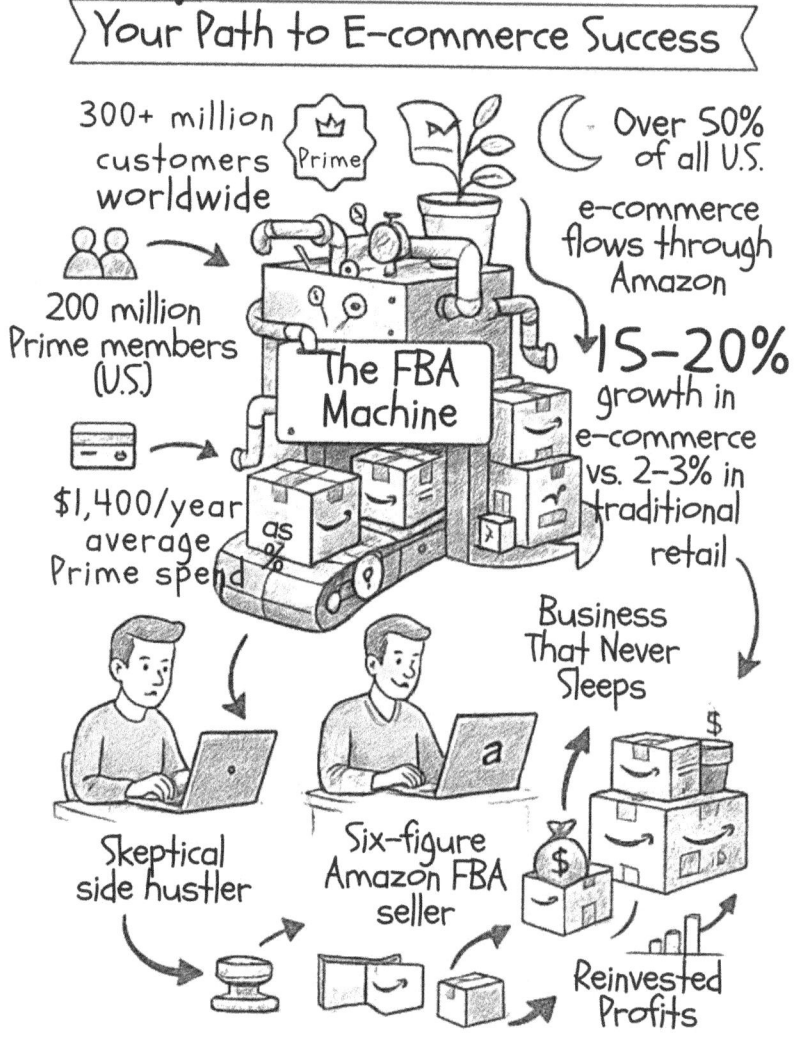

Chapter 1: Why Amazon FBA?

Why FBA is Your Gateway to E-commerce Success

What makes Amazon FBA particularly attractive for beginners is that we can leverage Amazon's world-class fulfillment infrastructure from day one:

- Multibillion-dollar warehouse network
- Sophisticated inventory management system
- Established base of over 300 million active buyers
- World-class shipping and logistics
- 24/7 customer service
- Trusted returns process

With FBA, we find the products and ship them to Amazon's warehouses. Amazon then handles storage, packing, shipping, customer service, returns—even Prime shipping benefits. It's like renting the infrastructure of a Fortune 500 company to power your small business.

This allows you to start small, testing products with minimal risk, and scaling as you gain confidence. Many successful sellers began with just a few hundred dollars and a couple hours per week.

P.A.T.H. - *Prospect. Assess. Test. Harvest*

Compare this to a traditional retail business with its massive startup costs and overhead.

Moreover, Amazon's FBA infrastructure gives you instant credibility. Your products appear right alongside major brands, eligible for Prime shipping, backed by Amazon's renowned service. To customers, you're as legitimate as any major retailer on the platform.

Chapter 1: Why Amazon FBA?

> **PRO TIP:**
> Focus on leveraging Amazon's infrastructure rather than building your own – you're renting a Fortune 100 company's capabilities from day one.

P.A.T.H. - Prospect. Assess. Test. Harvest

Leveraging Amazon's Delivery Network

Amazon has spent billions creating a distribution network where products can reach 95% of U.S. customers within two days. This opens opportunities to compete not just on price, but on convenience.

A fellow seller shared an amazing insight that changed how we think about selling on Amazon. While it might seem like we're competing with millions of other sellers, Amazon's delivery system actually creates endless local opportunities. It's a lot like pizza delivery – we're not competing with every pizza shop in the country, just the ones that can deliver hot pizza in our customer's neighborhood. Amazon works similarly. Even though there are millions of sellers on Amazon, you're really only competing with those who have products available in the same neighborhood. This makes success on Amazon much more achievable than most people think.

Prime members frequently prioritize convenience over significant price differences. They'll often choose items they can receive quickly over less expensive options with longer delivery times. While you can't control where

Chapter 1: Why Amazon FBA?

Amazon chooses to distribute your inventory, you can at least trust Amazon's ability to put inventory where the customer demand is.

CHAPTER 1
RESOURCES
and
IMPLEMENTATION TOOLS

Chapter 1: Why Amazon FBA?

Resources and Implementation Tools

To help you put these concepts into action, we've prepared several resources available at

OfficialOlsons.com

Essential Downloads:

✓ Amazon FBA Quick-Start Checklist

✓ P.A.T.H. framework Implementation Guide

✓ Amazon Seller Glossary

Bonus Materials:

- Initial investment planning worksheet

Next Steps:

1. Complete the Quick-Start Checklist
2. Review the P.A.T.H. framework Guide
3. Set your 30-day startup goals

Chapter 2: Keepa the Story Straight

P.A.T.H. - Prospect. Assess. Test. Harvest

Chapter 2: Keepa the Story Straight

Have you ever wondered whether that Amazon deal is actually a bargain? Keepa is your secret weapon—your savvy, data-driven shopping companion. It acts like a relentless bargain hunter that never sleeps, tracking over 5 billion products across Amazon's marketplaces worldwide. Whether you're a smart shopper looking to stretch your budget or an Amazon reseller making strategic decisions, Keepa arms you with real-time and historical pricing insights that put you ahead of the game.

How Keepa Works

Getting started with Keepa is easy. You can visit its website directly, but the browser extension is where the magic happens. It seamlessly integrates into Amazon's product pages, overlaying detailed price history charts that instantly reveal whether a deal is truly a deal. No more guesswork, no more switching between tabs—Keepa keeps the story straight and saves you time.

But that's just the beginning. Behind the scenes, Keepa relentlessly monitors price changes across Amazon, tracking prices from Amazon itself, third-party sellers, and even warehouse deals. It's like

Chapter 2: Keepa the Story Straight

having a personal shopper who alerts you the moment prices drop on the products you want. Whether you're hunting for a bargain or maximizing resale profits, Keepa ensures you never miss an opportunity to save or earn.

Keepa for Consumers

Keepa transforms how you shop on Amazon, giving you insider knowledge about product pricing. Ever hesitated over whether to buy now or wait for a better price? Keepa's historical price charts show you exactly how a product's price has fluctuated, helping you spot real discounts and avoid fake "limited time" offers.

Even better, you can set custom alerts for price drops—no more refreshing pages or checking back constantly. Want that espresso machine at a steal? Set your ideal price, and Keepa notifies you the moment it hits your target.

Savvy shoppers love Keepa for its side-by-side seller comparisons. If you're comfortable buying from Amazon Warehouse or third-party sellers, Keepa lays out all the pricing options, including Prime vs. non-Prime pricing. For frequent buyers, this feature alone can save hundreds of dollars over time.

P.A.T.H. - Prospect. Assess. Test. Harvest

Here's a game-changer: Keepa lets you compare prices across Amazon marketplaces worldwide. With a click, Keepa reveals international price trends, giving you an edge in global shopping.

Whether you're planning a major purchase or just love scoring the best deals, Keepa turns you into a smart, strategic shopper who always buys at the right time.

Keepa for Resellers (Amazon FBA & Arbitrage Sellers)

If you sell on Amazon, Keepa is about to become your best friend. It's more than a price tracker—it's a market intelligence powerhouse that helps FBA sellers and retail arbitrage pros make smarter, more profitable decisions.

Know What Sells and When

Keepa's historical data doesn't just track prices - it helps you spot demand patterns. For some listings, sales rank history may still offers clues, but for clearer velocity signals, look for the 'Sold in Last 30 Days' data point when it's available..

Chapter 2: Keepa the Story Straight

Analyze the Competition Like a Pro

This is where Keepa truly shines. Imagine seeing exactly how many sellers have competed in a niche over time. Want to know when Amazon itself enters or exits the market? Keepa lays it all out.

With this "x-ray vision", you can track FBA vs. FBM trends, predict pricing shifts, and understand the competitive landscape before investing a single dollar.

Maximize Profitability

Selling on Amazon is focuses on profits, not just sales, and Keepa helps you stay ahead of price wars. You can:

- Track Buy Box patterns to see how Amazon and third-party sellers price their products.

- Set alerts for profit margins that account for Amazon fees—so you only invest in winners.

- Monitor coupon patterns and promotions to time your inventory purchases perfectly.

For serious sellers, Keepa's bulk data exports and API access provide deep-dive analytics, allowing for automated research and smarter sourcing.

P.A.T.H. - Prospect. Assess. Test. Harvest

Keepa's Power Features

For data-driven sellers and tech-savvy users, Keepa offers next-level tools:

- API Access – Tap into Keepa's vast database to build custom tools or integrate it into your workflows.

- Global Price Tracking – Compare prices across multiple countries

- "Freemium" Model – Basic price tracking is free, while advanced analytics cost a small monthly fee—a fraction of what it saves you in smarter sourcing.

Mastering Keepa Without Overwhelm

At first glance, Keepa can seem overwhelming—with billions of products tracked and countless data points, it's easy to fall into analysis paralysis. But here's the secret:

You don't need to master every feature.

By focusing on just three key metrics (which we'll cover in the next chapters), you'll gain a solid foundation for profitable sourcing and be able to make a testing decision. Like driving a car—you

Chapter 2: Keepa the Story Straight

don't need to know how the engine works to get where you're going.

Master the essentials first, and as you gain confidence, Keepa will become your most powerful tool for making data-driven decisions—whether you're scoring deals or scaling your reselling business.

CHAPTER 2
RESOURCES
and
IMPLEMENTATION TOOLS

Chapter 2: Keepa the Story Straight

Resources and Implementation Tools

To help you put these concepts into action, we've prepared several resources available at

OfficialOlsons.com/path

Essential Downloads:

✓ Keepa account setup checklist

Bonus Materials:

- Keepa analysis video tutorials
- Keepa account setup guide
- Data interpretation examples

Next Steps:

1. Set up your Keepa account
2. Review sample listings

Chapter 3: The Prospect Phase

Chapter 3: The Prospect Phase

Building Your Base

Imagine you're about to build your dream house. You wouldn't start by picking out curtains or choosing paint colors, would you? Of course not. You'd focus first on creating a rock-solid foundation. Building an Amazon FBA business works the same way, and don't worry if you've never sold anything online before—we'll walk you through every step.

Your foundation begins with what we call the **Prospect Phase.** Identifying and gathering Amazon listings that you can sell within compliance of Amazon's guidelines. We call these ASINs. An ASIN (Amazon Standard Identification Number) is Amazon's unique product identifier, like a social security number for each item on Amazon. Every listing has one, and it's your key to tracking and managing potential opportunities.

Chapter 3: The Prospect Phase

The Pre-Flight Inspection: Your First Line of Defense

Every week, we encounter enthusiastic new sellers who share a remarkably similar story. Despite investing thousands of dollars, their initial excitement turns to disappointment because they skipped crucial evaluation steps. It's usually not their fault! They don't know what they don't know and, unfortunately, most of these sellers typically discover us AFTER learning expensive lessons about the importance of thorough product research.

The pattern is consistent: attracted by seemingly perfect listings showing strong sales and profit potential, they rush into inventory purchases without conducting proper due diligence. It's like buying a house based only on the online photos - everything might look perfect in the carefully staged pictures, but without a proper inspection, you could miss serious structural issues that end up costing thousands.

This recurring scenario led us to develop our **Pre-Flight Inspection** process. Just as pilots use systematic checklists to ensure safe flights, successful Amazon sellers need a thorough system for evaluating potential.

P.A.T.H. - Prospect. Assess. Test. Harvest

products. Through years of working with thousands of sellers, we've identified the critical checkpoints that consistently separate successful product launches from costly mistakes.

Chapter 3: The Prospect Phase

Pre-Flight Inspection
Your First Line of Defense

Check the Brand Field

Listing Title
Listing Image
Listing Brand Field

Be the Brand Detective

Don't Skip the Checklist

Check Before You Ship

A misbranded listing can be tempting, but don't trust it. It could get you into trouble with Amazon and/or the brand.

P.A.T.H. - Prospect. Assess. Test. Harvest

Brand Consistency: Your First Critical Check

Think of yourself as a detective when examining a candidate listing. Don't worry if you've never done this before, we'll show you exactly what to look for. Open any Amazon listing and let's walk through it together:

1. First, scroll down to the "Product information" section. Find the "Brand" field. This is your baseline—the official brand name.

2. Now, look at the product title at the top of the page. Does the brand name match exactly? Not just similar, but exactly?

3. Examine the product images. Look at any packaging or labels shown. Again, does the brand name match perfectly?

One of our newest students, barely a week into learning our system, was reviewing a listing where the brand field showed "Tech-Pro," but the product images showed "TechPro Solutions" on the packaging. This might seem like a tiny difference, just a hyphen and the word "Solutions", but catching this small detail saved her from potential authentication troubles down the road. These might include compliance difficulties, as well as customer satisfaction issues.

Chapter 3: The Prospect Phase

PRO TIP:
When the brand field is not obvious on a listing, use the Keepa extension and navigate to the Data tab and then Product Details to find the exact brand field.

P.A.T.H. - Prospect. Assess. Test. Harvest

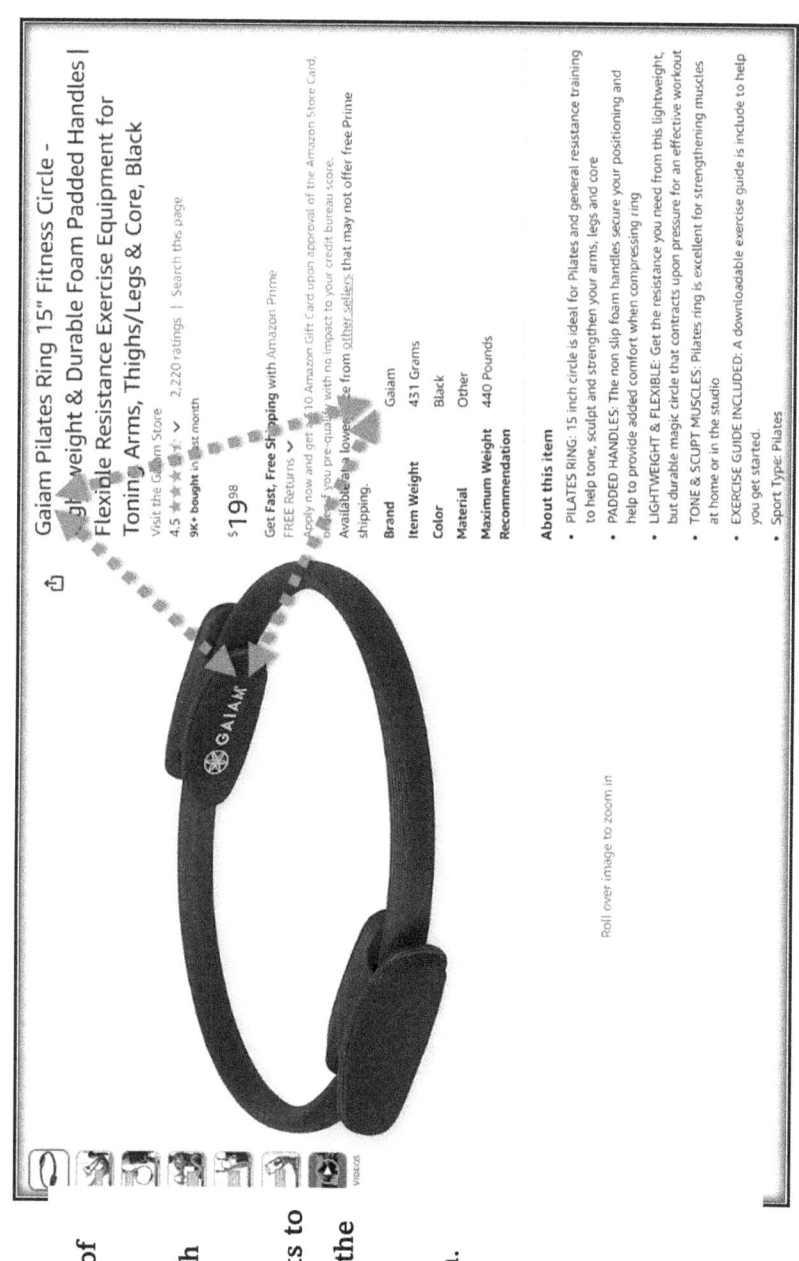

Example of Amazon listing with matching data points to complete the pre-flight inspection.

Chapter 3: The Prospect Phase

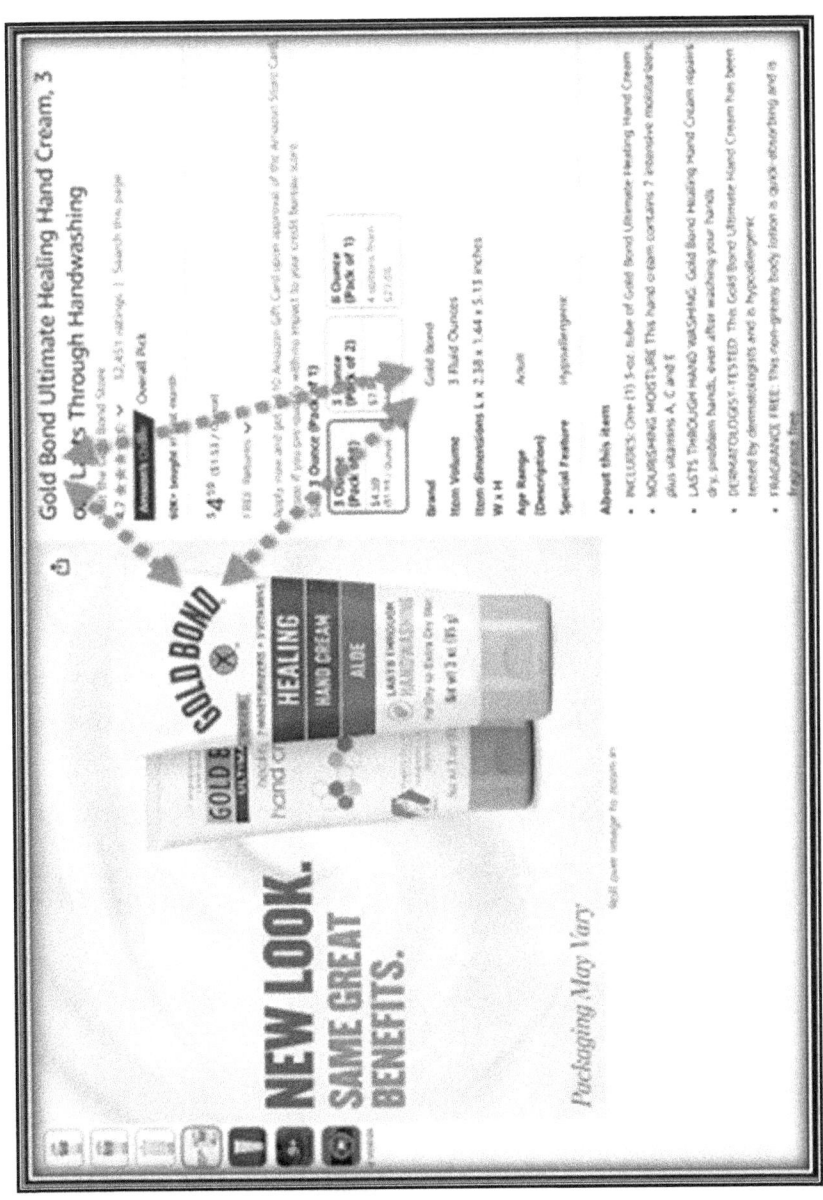

Example of Amazon listing with matching data points to complete the pre-flight inspection.

P.A.T.H. - Prospect. Assess. Test. Harvest

Example of an Amazon listing that does not pass the pre-flight inspection.

Chapter 3: The Prospect Phase

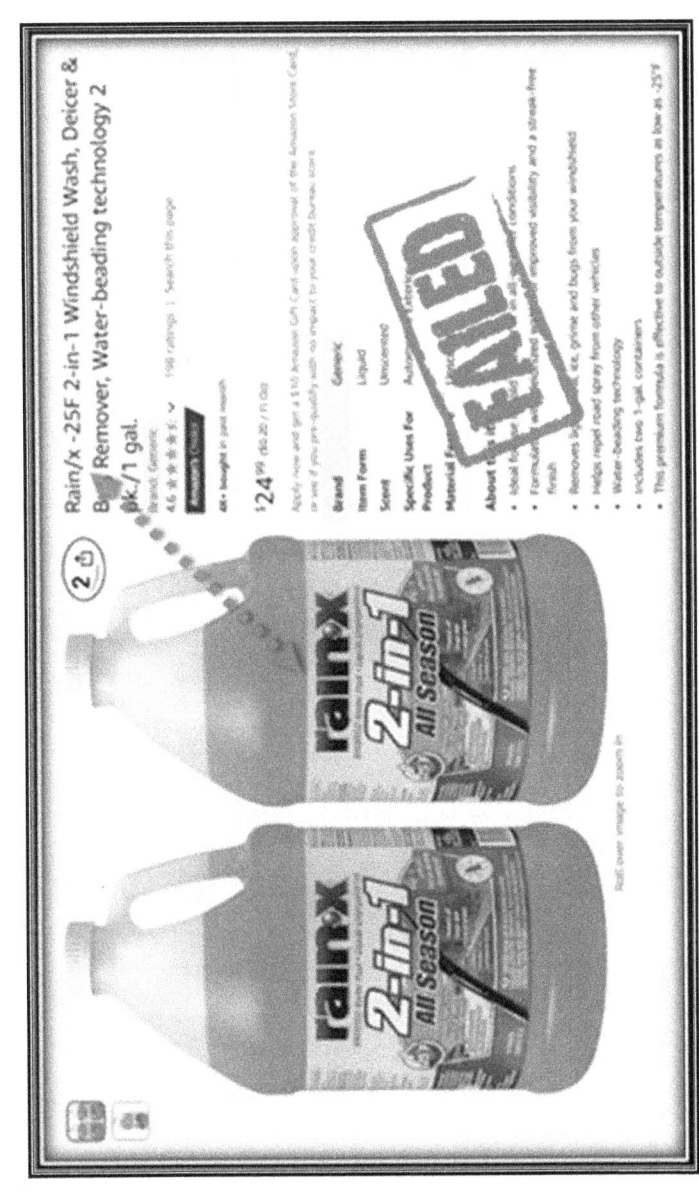

Example of an Amazon listing that does not pass the pre-flight inspection.

P.A.T.H. - Prospect. Assess. Test. Harvest

Use the Keepa extension's Data tab, Product Details, to view the brand field as it was entered into Amazon.

Chapter 3: The Prospect Phase

Listing Verification: Your Protection Process

Next, let's talk about the accuracy of a listing—it's sort of like your product's DNA. It may sound complex, but this is much simpler than it sounds. A recent workshop attendee, starting with very little Amazon experience, showed how powerful basic verification can be.

During their first week of product research, they were examining grocery category listings when they caught a critical detail that many overlook: the product images and description didn't match. While the main image showed a 16-ounce package, the description listed 14 ounces. This kind of careful validation, which we emphasize in our training, helps prevent inventory mistakes before they happen.

Here's how you can do the same kind of review:

- Look at the main product image
- Read the product title carefully
- Check the bullet points
- Review the product description
- Examine all other images

P.A.T.H. - Prospect. Assess. Test. Harvest

If you notice any differences—even small ones—it's likely best to move on to another listing. Remember, you're not really limited on choices. The Amazon.com platform has well over a billion listings. That's just in the United States. Let's take a moment to think about how many listings that is. If you were to spend one second looking at each of a million listings, it would take you a little over 11 days. That does not include sleep or potty breaks. If you were to spend one second on each of a billion listings, it would take you almost 32 years. That's a lot to choose from so don't get tied up in a confusing or problematic listing. Go find another.

Like learning any new skill, your first attempts at **Pre-Flight Inspection** might feel slow, clunky and uncertain. You might spend several minutes on a single listing, carefully cross-checking every detail. That's perfectly normal—in fact, it's exactly where most successful sellers start. We've watched countless workshop participants transform from spending 5-10 minutes evaluating a single listing to confidently assessing opportunities in seconds. This expertise doesn't happen overnight; it comes from lots of practice and reviewing hundreds of listings to develop that pattern recognition skill.

It's a lot like learning to drive a car. Remember how overwhelming it felt to monitor your speed, watch your mirrors, maintain your lane position,

Chapter 3: The Prospect Phase

remember when to use the blinker, remember your route and track other vehicles all at once? Yet today, you probably do all of that automatically. The same natural progression happens with listing evaluation. Your brain starts to develop a pattern recognition that makes spotting discrepancies almost intuitive.

One of our workshop attendees kept track of her progress during her first month. Her first listing evaluation took 12 minutes. By week two, she averaged 7 minutes per listing. By the end of the month, she could confidently evaluate most listings in 2-3 minutes. Today, she can often spot critical issues within seconds of opening a listing. This isn't because she's cutting corners—it's because she's trained her eye to zero in on the essential details and evaluates them against the set of criteria outlined here.

So be patient with yourself as you develop this skill. Take as much time as you need on each listing in the beginning. Focus on accuracy rather than speed. The efficiency will come naturally with practice, and one day soon, you'll surprise yourself by spotting a brand inconsistency or specification mismatch almost instantly. This is a skill that pays dividends throughout your Amazon FBA journey, so the time you invest in mastering it now will reward you many times over.

P.A.T.H. - *Prospect. Assess. Test. Harvest*

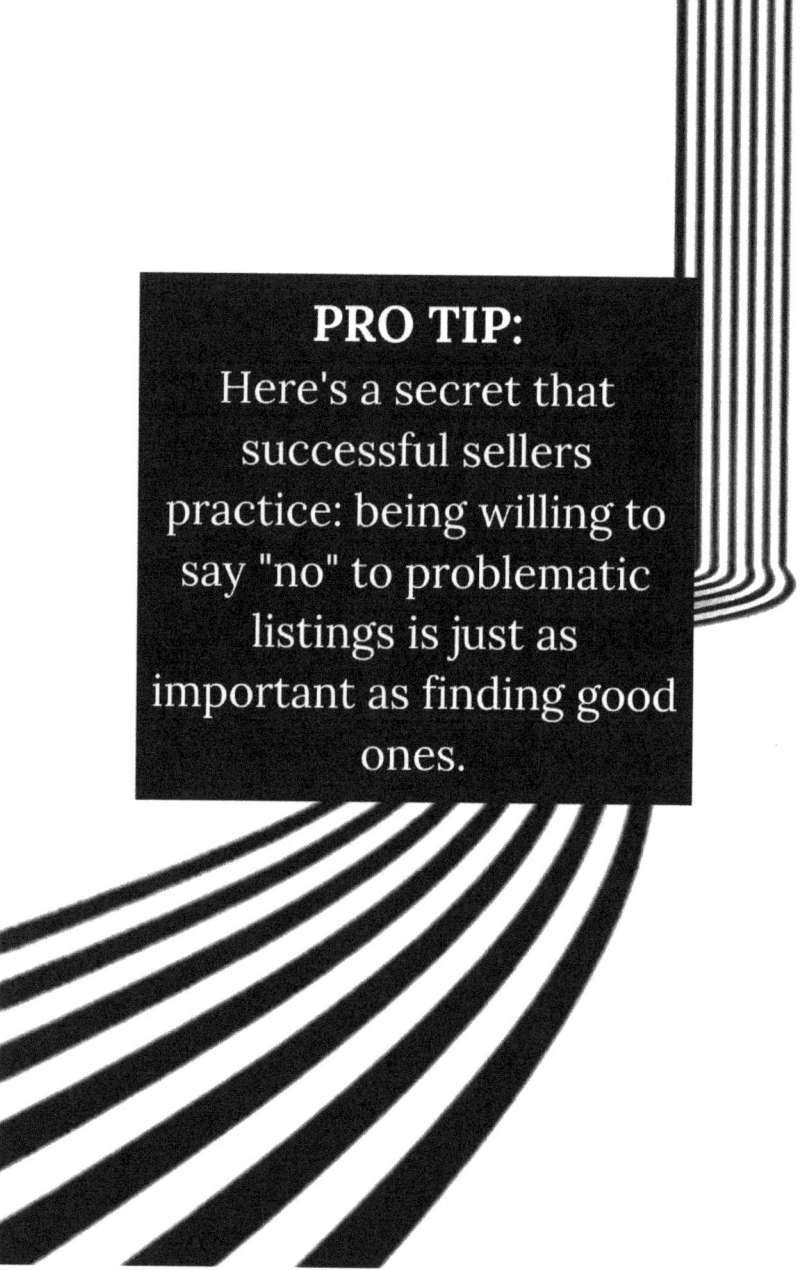

PRO TIP:
Here's a secret that successful sellers practice: being willing to say "no" to problematic listings is just as important as finding good ones.

Chapter 3: The Prospect Phase

Bridging the Gap: Matching listings with Suppliers

Let's talk about something that often scares new sellers: finding reliable, authorized suppliers. We call this crucial step **Bridging the Gap**, and there's a reason for that name. It's the bridge between finding an attractive listing and having a legitimate supplier for the product you would like to sell. And like any bridge, you need to be certain it's solid before you cross it.

Let us be crystal clear about something important: while we can automate many aspects of reselling on Amazon, along with listing analysis, supplier verification typically requires human judgment. It's that critical step that can separate successful, compliant sellers from those who end up with account risks or suspended listings. We've seen too many sellers learn this lesson the hard way, trusting automated tools or shortcuts only to face serious consequences later.

We see this fear of supplier sourcing in every workshop we conduct—that unmistakable nervous energy that fills the room when someone finally raises their hand and asks, "But where do I actually get the products?" You can feel the tension as everyone leans in, hoping for some secret wholesale directory or magic supplier list. If you're feeling this anxiety, you're not alone. Most sellers who have found success started with the same question.

The Simple Solution Hiding in Plain Sight

Here's a secret that might surprise you—and maybe even relieve some of that pressure: some of the best suppliers are places where you probably shopped this week. Yes, those same retail stores you visit regularly can become your most reliable sourcing partners. They've already done much of the hard work for you by verifying their supply chains, maintaining manufacturer relationships, ensuring product authenticity, and providing clear documentation.

Think about your local Target, Walmart, or Costco. These aren't just stores; they're potential goldmines for your Amazon business. And here's what might really surprise you: this isn't just a "beginner's strategy" that you'll outgrow. Our own FBA business still sources almost exclusively from these same retail stores. We've tried all the fancy approaches—direct importing, manufacturer relationships, exclusive distributor deals—but we keep coming back to retail sourcing because it just works.

Chapter 3: The Prospect Phase

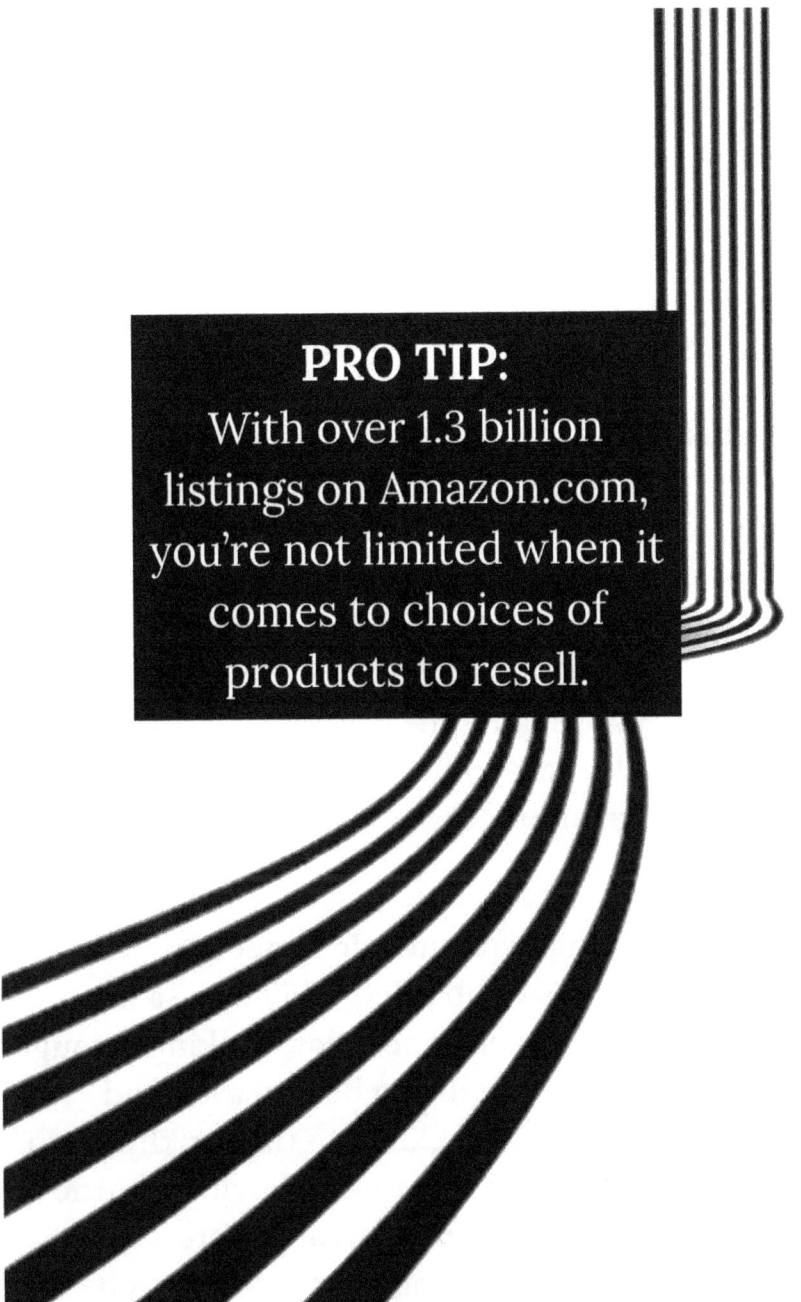

PRO TIP:
With over 1.3 billion listings on Amazon.com, you're not limited when it comes to choices of products to resell.

P.A.T.H. - Prospect. Assess. Test. Harvest

The Power of Retail Arbitrage

"But how can you make money buying retail and selling retail?" We hear this question all the time, usually asked with a mix of skepticism and curiosity. Let us explain the concept of arbitrage. Don't let that fancy financial term scare you. It simply means buying something in one market and selling it in another where it could be worth more.

Let's bring this to life with something we can all understand: bottled water. The same exact bottle might cost $1.69 at your local grocery store, $2.75 at the gas station convenience store, and a whopping $6.25 or more at the airport. In fact, we were recently at a resort where a bottle of water was selling for $14! Meanwhile, you can get that same bottle in bulk at a warehouse club for a fraction of these other retail prices. So, what's the difference? Convenience.

Think about what you must do to get that rock-bottom warehouse club price - driving to a huge store, parking in an enormous lot, walking through a massive warehouse, lifting heavy cases, and lugging them to the checkout, to the car, then into your home. Now compare that to buying a bottle of water at the airport. You're already there, you're thirsty, and you can't bring your own through security. For many, the convenience is worth the

Chapter 3: The Prospect Phase

extra cost (especially when we forget to bring our refillable water bottles).

This is exactly where your Amazon FBA opportunity comes in. Many of Amazon's customers are paying for convenience—shopping from their couch, not driving to stores, avoiding parking hassles, skipping out on the heavy lifting, with delivery right to their door, often on the same day! They're not just buying the product; they're buying the entire convenient shopping experience, and they are willing to pay for it.

P.A.T.H. - *Prospect. Assess. Test. Harvest*

> "Today millions of Amazon shoppers will pay LESS than they were willing to for items that will arrive SLOWER than they'd prefer all because sellers LIKE YOU AND ME failed to stock the warehouse nearest the buyer with the most in demand items being sold on Amazon."
>
> -Jim Cockrum, Silent Sales Machine

Chapter 3: The Prospect Phase

A Demonstrated Path to Success

Remember Jeff Bezos's start? He didn't begin with a sophisticated distribution network—he was buying books from local bookstores and selling them online from a garage. He understood something fundamental: people will pay more for convenience. He was practicing retail arbitrage before most people had ever heard the term.

And here's the really encouraging part: this model works even better today. The recent pandemic has dramatically increased people's appreciation for convenient shopping options. Many customers now prefer to shop online even when items might cost more. You don't need to feel guilty about your prices or apologize for the markup. You're providing a valuable service by making products available to a wider market with the convenience of same-day, next-day or 2-day delivery.

Starting Smart: The Golden Rule

Let us share something we wish someone had told us when we started: you need to flip the usual thinking process on its head. Many new sellers fall into what we call the "perfect listing trap" - they find an Amazon listing that looks amazing, get excited about all the potential profit, and then spend countless hours trying to track down a way to source it or to find it for pennies cheaper. Here's our golden rule: a perfect listing means nothing if you can't source the product reliably and compliantly. It's not unlike finding your dream house on Zillow, only to discover it was sold last month. No matter how perfect that house looks, if it's not actually available, it's just a pretty picture.

Here's a scenario we see play out repeatedly when we coach: an enthusiastic seller becomes fixated on a seemingly perfect product, showing exceptional margins and strong sales history. After spending three weeks contacting numerous wholesalers and researching overseas suppliers, they hit the common roadblock - the brand only worked through an exclusive distribution network closed to new sellers. This valuable time could have been invested in finding and testing products with legitimate sourcing opportunities.

Or, how about a story of our own?

> Brian: I remember falling in love with a candy product in the early days of building our Amazon FBA business. I had found a few candy-type products that were working ok for us. Then, I found this tub of rock candy on a stick. I just knew that this product was going to be a home run! I knew it because I saw many listings with similar rock candy on a

Chapter 3: The Prospect Phase

stick and they appeared to be selling very well.

I had initially found a retail source for the product but the price I would pay would not leave any room for profits. So, I spent the next 3-4 weeks trying to track down a supplier with a better cost. I even went so far as to make connections overseas and got a quote for a final price that would provide potential profits. There was just one problem – I would have to buy a shipping container full (~5,000 units) that would come to the US on a large ship and I would have to work out the details around importing laws, taxes, compliance issues, transport to a warehouse, etc.

On the one hand I felt kind of like I had won because I had completed the mission of finding a better price. However, on the other hand, because I was not realistically in a position to complete the process, I had essentially wasted all of that time acting like Sherlock Holmes for a product I would not be able to complete the purchase on. I could have spent those weeks focusing on real opportunities.

P.A.T.H. - Prospect. Assess. Test. Harvest

Your Road Ahead

This approach might seem too simple, like - there must be some catch. But sometimes the best solutions are the simplest ones. While other new sellers get tangled up in complex sourcing strategies or risk their accounts with questionable suppliers and/or listings, you can build a solid foundation using proven, legitimate sources that are hiding in plain sight. The key is understanding that **Bridging the Gap** isn't finding the most exotic or exclusive suppliers—it's finding reliable, verifiable sources that allow you to sell with confidence on Amazon. When you start with familiar retail stores, you're not just buying inventory; you're building a sustainable business foundation that can grow and evolve as your experience increases.

PRO TIP:

Don't overlook retail stores as reliable suppliers. While many sellers chase complex sourcing strategies, national and regional chains offer a simple, proven path to start. We like to remind clients we work with of a quote from Codie Sanchez who says, "Complexity makes you seem smart. Simplicity makes you money." So, if you've been losing sleep over supplier sourcing, take a deep breath. The path forward might be simpler and more accessible than you imagined.

P.A.T.H. - Prospect. Assess. Test. Harvest

The Retail Sourcing Strategy: Starting Where You're Comfortable

One of our coaching clients, who started her Amazon adventure with zero business experience, was nervous about contacting manufacturers and wholesalers (like many beginners are), so we showed her a different approach.

In the early days of her Amazon journey, she started building relationships with managers at her local department stores. You might be thinking, "Wait, can I really build an Amazon business buying from retail stores?" The answer is a resounding yes!

Here's what she discovered:

1. Retail sourcing eliminated common beginner hurdles:

- No complicated negotiations
- No minimum order quantities
- No international shipping hassles
- No worries about product authenticity

2. She could start small and scale up naturally:

- Begin with just a few items
- Test different products easily

Chapter 3: The Prospect Phase

- Learn the Amazon platform with minimal risk
- Build confidence through small successes

Even more surprising? She found that large retailers' massive buying power often meant their retail prices were lower than what she could get directly from manufacturers, wholesalers or distributors. Instead of competing with their volume-based discounts, she decided to leverage them.

Building Retail Relationships: A Beginner's Guide

Here's how she built relationships with store managers, and how you can too:

Start Simple:

- Visit stores during slower hours
- Introduce yourself politely
- Be honest about your Amazon business (we're not doing anything wrong here)
- Ask about store policies
- Show genuine interest in building a long-term relationship

P.A.T.H. - Prospect. Assess. Test. Harvest

As your relationship grows:

- Maintain consistent purchasing patterns
- Always be professional and courteous
- Keep your commitments
- Express appreciation for their help

Today, store managers actually contact her about upcoming sales, hold products for her, and sometimes even order specific quantities just for her business. Remember, everyone starts as a beginner—what matters is taking that first step.

Chapter 3: The Prospect Phase

Your VIABLE ASIN Database: Keeping It Simple

Now we're getting to what we consider the crown jewel of the **Prospect Phase**: your VIABLE ASIN database. Don't let the term "database" intimidate you—this can be as simple as a spreadsheet or even a notebook when you're starting out.

Robin Joy: Let me share something I see happening all too often in working with sellers: a newer seller opens their laptop, creates a spreadsheet, and proceeds to build what looks more like a NASA control panel than a business tracking system. We get it—when you're starting something new, especially something as exciting as an Amazon business, you want to do it "right." You want to track every possible metric, record every tiny detail, and feel like you're on top of everything.

But here's the truth we've learned from watching hundreds of sellers succeed (and struggle): complexity is often the enemy of progress. The principle is simple - done is better than perfect. We frequently see this play out in our one-on-one coaching, where enthusiastic sellers sometimes create unnecessarily complex systems.

P.A.T.H. - Prospect. Assess. Test. Harvest

In one memorable instance, a participant developed an intricate tracking system with 47 different data points for each ASIN, monitoring everything from historical prices to market depth. The inevitable result? The system proved too cumbersome to maintain, and within two weeks, they stopped using it entirely. This experience clearly illustrates why simpler systems often lead to better outcomes.

That's why we advocate for keeping it radically simple. Focus on just three essential pieces of information:

1. ASIN (you can copy this right from the Amazon listing)

2. Supplier information (where you can get it)

3. Cost (what you'll pay for it)

"But wait," you might be thinking, "what about all those other important metrics?" Here's the beautiful thing—Amazon already tracks most of that information for you. Price history? There are tools for that. Sales velocity? You can check that anytime. Market depth? That data is always current on the listing. You don't need to maintain a historical record of constantly changing data that you can look up in seconds when you need it.

Chapter 3: The Prospect Phase

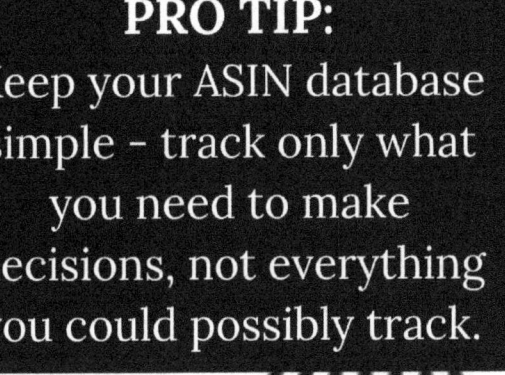

PRO TIP:
Keep your ASIN database simple - track only what you need to make decisions, not everything you could possibly track.

P.A.T.H. - Prospect. Assess. Test. Harvest

When checking the weather, you don't keep a daily log of temperature, humidity, and wind speed (unless you're my grandpa!). When you need that information, you just look it up. It's the same with Amazon metrics—track only what you actually need to make decisions, not what might be interesting to know. In the chapter on the **3-Step Check** we will show you how few data points you really need to review in order to make a decision to test.

The dangers of overcomplication go beyond just wasted time. We've seen sellers:

- Get so caught up in tracking competitive data that they miss actual selling opportunities

- Spend hours updating spreadsheets instead of sourcing products

- Become paralyzed by analysis, always feeling like they need "just a bit more data" before taking action

- Burn out from the overwhelming task of maintaining complex systems

- Lose sight of the basic principles that actually drive profit

A workshop participant proved that simplicity can lead to success. Starting with nothing more than a phone app for a thriving six-figure business in just

Chapter 3: The Prospect Phase

six months. Meanwhile, other sellers who created elaborate tracking systems were still tweaking formulas and adjusting spreadsheets. This success story highlights one of our core principles: the best system isn't the most complex - it's the one you'll actually use every day.

So, give yourself permission to keep it simple. You can always add more complexity later if you genuinely need it. But in our experience, most sellers find that these few basic pieces of information, consistently tracked, provide everything they need to build a successful Amazon business. Focus your energy on finding and testing products rather than building elaborate tracking systems. After all, you make money by selling products, not by maintaining spreadsheets.

Making Your Database Work Smarter

Here's a clever tracking strategy we learned from one of our coaching clients. They add two simple but powerful elements to their basic tracking:

> 1. Quick notes about why certain ASINs didn't qualify for testing Example: "Seasonal item" or "Need to verify a new normal"

> 2. Review reminders Example: "Check again next month" or "Review after holiday season"

By revisiting these previously disqualified listings monthly, she's uncovered numerous profitable opportunities as market conditions shifted. This simple practice transforms her database from a static list into a dynamic opportunity pipeline.

Putting It All Together

Think of the **Prospect Phase** as laying the cornerstone of your Amazon business. Every VIABLE ASIN you identify and every supplier relationship you build is an investment in your future success. When you're ready to move to the **Assessment Phase** (which we'll cover in the next chapter), you want to be choosing from a pool of

Chapter 3: The Prospect Phase

pre-qualified opportunities, not starting your search from scratch.

Remember this: the most successful Amazon sellers aren't necessarily the ones who move fastest, they're the ones who build the strongest foundations leveraging frameworks, systems, processes and discipline. Your Pre-Flight Inspection process, supplier relationships, and VIABLE ASIN database are the cornerstones of that foundation.

It's okay if all of this feels overwhelming at first. Everyone starts at ground zero, and you're already ahead of the game by learning these fundamentals. Take it one step at a time, and before you know it, you'll be spotting opportunities like a pro.

Ready to move on to Assessment? Let's keep building your P.A.T.H. to Amazon FBA success.

CHAPTER 3
RESOURCES
and
IMPLEMENTATION TOOLS

Resources and Implementation Tools

To help you put these concepts into action, we've prepared several resources available at

OfficialOlsons.com/path

Essential Downloads:

✓ **3-Step Check** Calculator

✓ VIABLE ASIN Database Template

Bonus Materials:

- Product research workflow guide
- Database management tutorials
- Supplier relationship scripts

Next Steps:

1. Set up your VIABLE ASIN database
2. Begin matching qualified ASINs with qualified sources

Chapter 4: The Assessment Phase

P.A.T.H. - Prospect. Assess. Test. Harvest

Chapter 4: The Assessment Phase

Using the 3-Step Check to Identify TESTABLE ASINs

Remember our conversation about building your dream house in Chapter 1? Now that you've laid that solid foundation by identifying VIABLE ASINs through your **Pre-Flight Inspection** and **Bridging the Gap** to authorized sources, it's time for the next exciting phase – deciding which rooms to build first. Think of the **Assessment Phase** as your building blueprint. You wouldn't start constructing every room in your house at once, right? The same goes for testing your VIABLE ASINs. We need a smart, systematic way to choose which opportunities to pursue first.

From Analysis Paralysis to Confident Action

Whether in coaching or at a workshop, we inevitably meet sellers caught up in analysis paralysis. One particularly memorable participant had spent three months buried in spreadsheets, analyzing different products, and second-guessing every decision. Despite identifying over 200 VIABLE

Chapter 4: The Assessment Phase

ASINs, they hadn't tested a single one - paralyzed by the fear of making a mistake. Does this sound familiar? That overwhelming desire to be absolutely certain before taking any action – we've all been there.

This common pattern of hesitation and over-analysis is exactly why we developed the **3-Step Check**. We wanted to eliminate that decision paralysis and give every seller a clear path forward. Think of it as your trusty GPS – you don't need to know every possible route to your destination; you just need to know the next turn to take.

The Birth of the 3-Step Check

It all started after we realized we didn't need to chase the Buy Box on a listing to get sales. We discovered the multidimensional nature of the Buy Box – how the same product can sell at different prices in different regions, how the Buy Box price changes many times during a given day. While this was exciting news, we noticed something important: experienced sellers could instinctively spot these opportunities, but newer sellers needed more guidance.

We asked ourselves: Could we create a simple system that would give newer sellers the same confidence as seasoned pros? Could we boil down the testing decision to just three straightforward yes-or-no questions? No "maybes", no "it depends," just clear, actionable criteria anyone could use.

What Really Matters When Testing?

In thinking about what we really need to know before testing a listing, we stripped away all the complexity and found three essential questions:

First, will this product sell quickly enough to give us meaningful data? Nobody wants their capital tied up for months waiting to make a decision. We've seen this lesson learned the hard way many times in our workshops, including one memorable example where a participant sent in Halloween products in April. Despite promising numbers on paper, they had to wait months to gather enough data to make any meaningful decisions about the product's viability.

Second, can we protect our investment? Even if the test doesn't work out exactly as we would like, we want evidence that we can at least get our money back in a worst-case scenario. We know there are no guarantees – nothing in business is guaranteed – but we can make smart, calculated decisions that are supported by evidence from historical data. We don't want to just start lighting twenty-dollar bills on fire.

Third, is there real potential for profit? After all, that's why we're doing this – to make money.

The 3-Step Check: Your Decision-Making GPS

In Chapter 1 we talked about keeping things simple, right? Well, the **3-Step Check** follows that same principle. Instead of drowning in data, we're going to focus on just three straightforward questions:

1. **Velocity**: Will this product sell quickly enough to give us meaningful test results?

2. **Capital Protection**: Do we have evidence that we can protect our investment?

3. **Profit Potential**: Is there possibility for a positive return?

That's all there is to it. Three simple yes-or-no questions that will tell you whether an ASIN is worth testing (a TESTABLE ASIN). No complex formulas, no advanced degrees required – just clear, straightforward answers that anyone can understand.

P.A.T.H. - *Prospect. Assess. Test. Harvest*

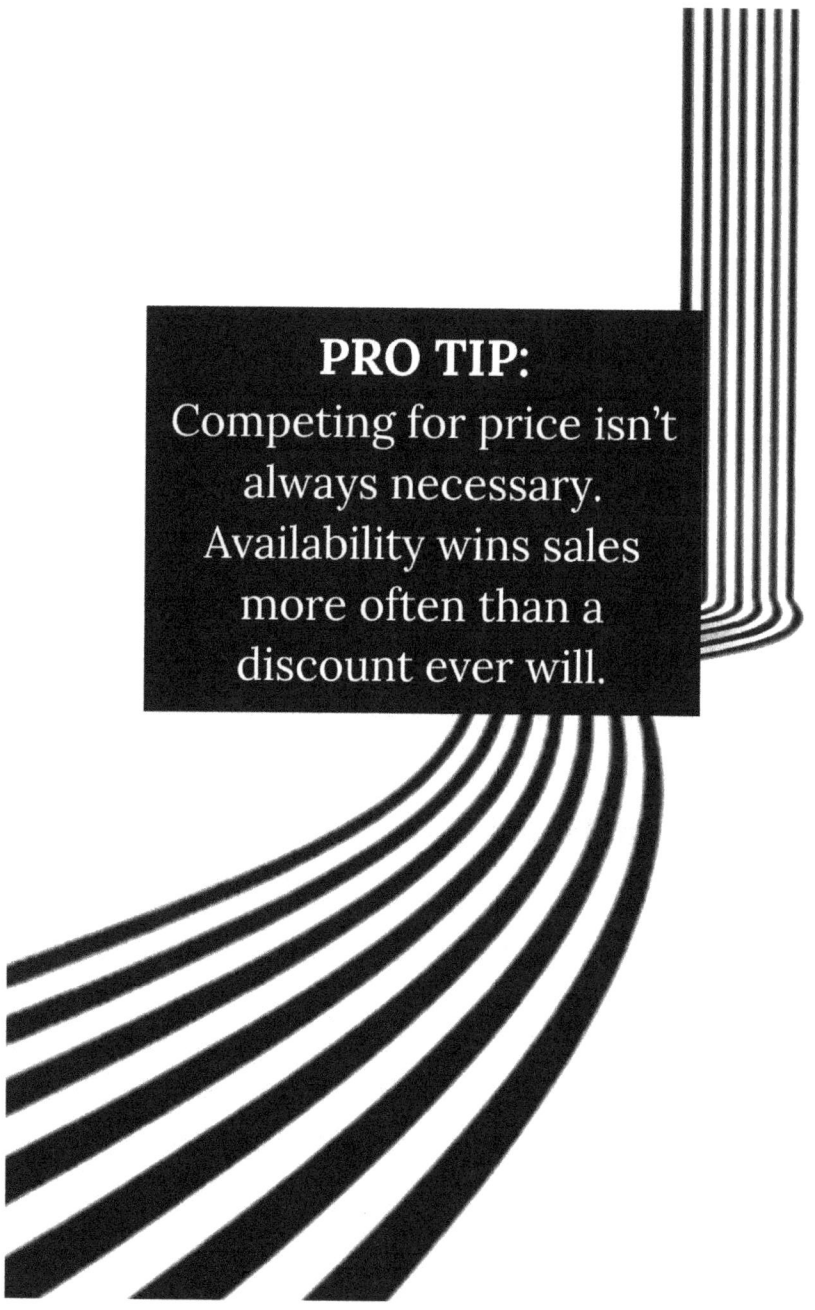

PRO TIP:
Competing for price isn't always necessary. Availability wins sales more often than a discount ever will.

Chapter 4: The Assessment Phase

Step 1: The Velocity Check Your First Green Light

The first problem we needed to solve was time. We'd seen too many sellers get stuck with slow-moving inventory; their capital tied up for months while they waited to see if a product would work out. That's why we made Velocity our first check.

Our accelerator program regularly reveals how sellers overcomplicate their initial analysis. One participant's journey particularly helped us refine our teaching approach. Like many beginners, they created elaborate spreadsheets and complex formulas, believing successful product selection required intensive mathematical analysis. Sound familiar?

The transformation came when we simplified Step 1 down to a single question: Has this ASIN sold enough recently to give us test-worthy data? The clearest signal today is the "Sold in Last 30 Days" number, shown on many listings. If it shows 50 units or more, that's your first green light. That volume gives you a realistic chance of getting in and out within 30–45 days which is fast enough to learn something without tying up capital too long.

"But why a minimum of 50?" Through hands-on coaching with hundreds of sellers, we've seen that this level of recent activity tends to produce usable data quickly, even if you're not the only seller. It's especially important for seasonal items. Sellers who test too early (or too late) often wait months for feedback. A 50-sale minimum gives you a time-tested filter to avoid stalls and learn fast.

Chapter 4: The Assessment Phase

*Don't overthink it.
Just answer yes or no.*

P.A.T.H. - Prospect. Assess. Test. Harvest

Understanding Keepa: Your Market Research Assistant

Keepa is the only tool that we really think you need to use this framework. There are some other tools like on-page calculators that can make quicker work of it, but they are optional and can be obtained later. Remember, Keepa is your personal market research assistant who's been watching every product 24/7. It shows you everything about a product's pricing history – the Buy Box price over time, FBA offer prices, even how long products maintain certain price points.

A common roadblock we encounter with those we work with involves Keepa analysis. When sellers first discover the wealth of data Keepa provides, many fall into the trap of thinking they need to understand and analyze every detail before moving forward. This is precisely the opposite of what we teach. Time and again, we watch participants delay action while trying to become Keepa experts, not realizing that mastery comes through practical application, not endless analysis.

The beauty of Keepa is that it does all the hard work for you, but – and this is crucial – we're only going to focus on what we absolutely need to know to start a test. Just like checking the weather before going outside. You don't need to know the barometric pressure, wind speed, and humidity levels – you just need to know if you should grab an umbrella or not.

A common breakthrough moment happens when our coaching clients realize they don't need to analyze every piece of data. While they often start by spending hours studying Keepa's graphs and statistics, they learn to zero in on what truly matters: Velocity, Capital Protection, and Profit Potential. This focused approach allows them to make faster decisions and spend more time taking action rather than getting lost in analysis.

Step 2: Capital Protection Your Safety Net

The second biggest fear we kept hearing from sellers was about losing money. Not just about missing out on profit, but about actually losing their investment. We saw people were having trouble pulling the trigger for a test because of this fear. That's why we made Capital Protection our second check. It's a whole lot easier to feel confident in the investment if you have a good chance of at least getting all your money back no matter what happens in the test. We know, especially when starting out, that we want to test as many products as we can so we can at least get that sale. If we can break even, we have the benefits of the sale even if we didn't make a profit.

A powerful transformation occurs in our programs when participants learn to overcome their initial fear of losing money. Many come to us with a decent amount of starting capital - often $5,000 or more - but remain frozen by the "what if I lose it all?" mindset that prevents so many potential sellers from moving forward.

We guide these participants to analyze Keepa's pricing history with a focus on Capital Protection rather than profit prediction. Did you catch that? We are not worried about how much profit, if any, there is when deciding to test, we will know that as a result of the test. We are simply wanting to test with an understanding of the worst that is likely to happen in the test. This practical approach involves a simple two-step process: first, calculate the true break-even price including all costs (product, shipping, Amazon fees). This is the price you would have to sell the item at to cover all of your investment plus selling fees which are taken out of proceeds at the time of sale. Then verify the product's history of maintaining prices above that threshold.

Here's the beautiful part about this approach: it alters the way our program participants think about

Chapter 4: The Assessment Phase

testing. They discover they don't need a guarantee of profit to start a

test – they just need evidence that they can protect their investment. When combined with small test quantities, this insight gives them the confidence to finally take action. After all, if they can recover their investment, they can capture all the other benefits of making sales, whether they profit or just break even.

P.A.T.H. - Prospect. Assess. Test. Harvest

FBA Seller Fees Breakdown

	32.99	Sell Price
−	4.95	Referral Fee (15.00%)
−	0.19	Monthly Storage Fee 30d / Jan - Sept
−	7.81	Fulfillment Fee
−	13.77	Buy Cost
−	2.26	Inbound Shipping Cost
=	4.02	Profit Estimated

Total Fees: $ 12.95 | **Total Cost:** $16.03 | **Total Fees & Cost:** $ 28.98

Example 1: the lowest possible sales price of a sample product that results in zero profit. (courtesy

Chapter 4: The Assessment Phase

Example 2: the same product from example 1 with increased sales price and increased referral fees with a gross profit. (courtesy asinzen.com)

FBA Seller Fees Breakdown

```
  28.26   Sell Price
-  4.24   Referral Fee (15.00%)
-  0.19   Monthly Storage Fee 30d / Jan - Sept
-  7.81   Fulfillment Fee
- 13.77   Buy Cost
-  2.26   Inbound Shipping Cost
=  0.00   Profit Estimated
```

Total Fees: $ 12.24| **Total Cost:** $16.03| **Total Fees & Cost:** $ 28.27

P.A.T.H. - *Prospect. Assess. Test. Harvest*

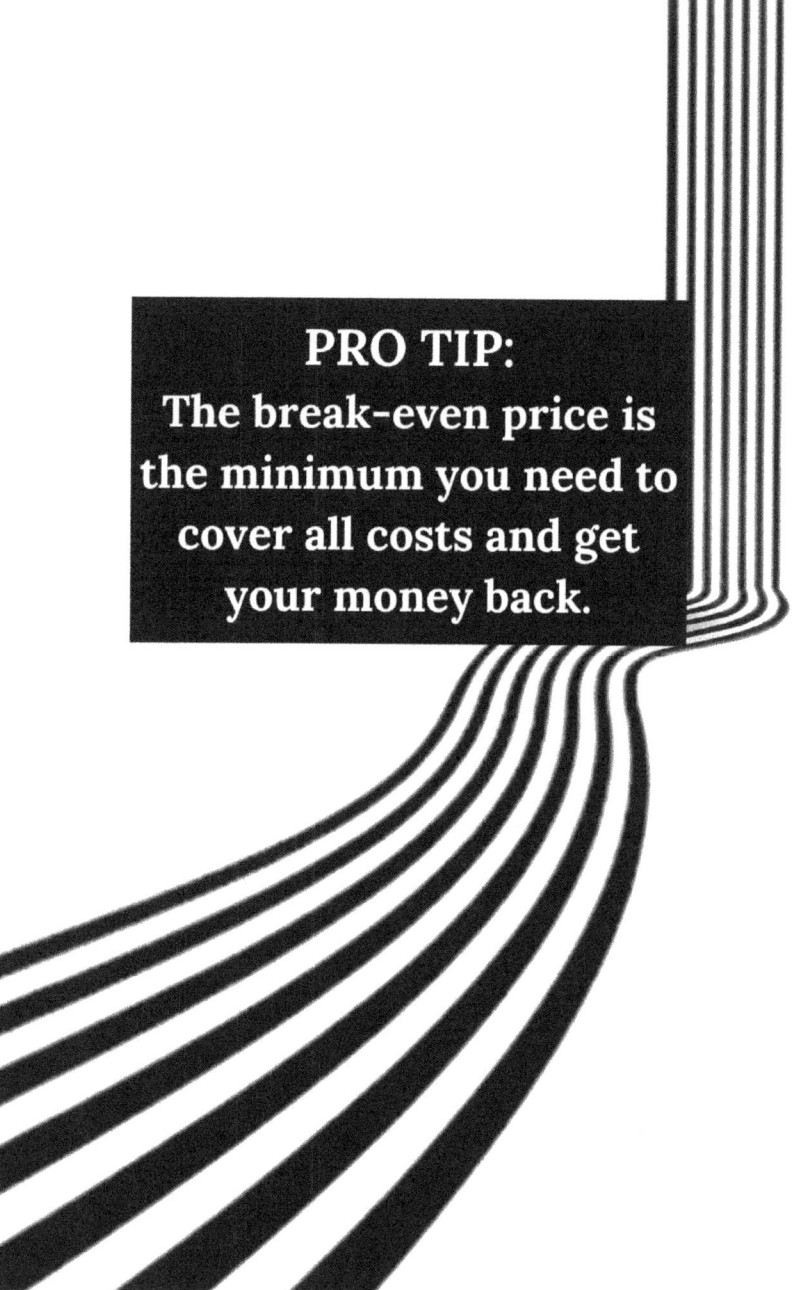

PRO TIP:
The break-even price is the minimum you need to cover all costs and get your money back.

Chapter 4: The Assessment Phase

DESIRED ROI	DESIRED PROFIT	EXPECTED SELL PRICE
0.00 %	$ 0.00	$ 0.00
0.03	0	28.27
6.29	1	29.45
18.75	3	31.8
31.22	5	34.15
43.73	7	36.51
62.45	10	40.04

Most on-page calculators include break-even and desired profit calculations as shown here for whole dollar profits (courtesy azinzen.com)

P.A.T.H. - Prospect. Assess. Test. Harvest

Step 3: Profit Potential
Your Growth Engine

Now, this third step might surprise you. When we were developing this system, we noticed something interesting: sellers who waited for perfect profit opportunities often ended up doing worse than those who were willing to test products with modest but realistic profit potential.

That's why we typically recommend looking for evidence of just a 15% or 20% Return on Investment (ROI) target. We can hear you now: "Only 20%? But I've seen YouTube videos promising 100% ROI or more!" Let us tell you why we settled on this number.

One of our accelerator program graduates drew on his knowledge professional fishing to illustrate this principle. Successful commercial fishermen, he noted, don't stake their entire day on landing one valuable tuna. Instead, they focus on consistently catching smaller fish that add up to significant profit over time. This approach allows them to build reliable income while remaining positioned for larger opportunities - a strategy that aptly mirrors successful Amazon selling.

This insight completely changed how we thought about profit potential. We realized we needed to

Chapter 4: The Assessment Phase

shift sellers' focus from hunting for perfect opportunities to building a portfolio of solid, reliable products. The 20% target made this possible – it was high enough to build a profitable business but low enough to find regular opportunities. That doesn't mean we turn away that big fish when we come across it, but it still must be tested for real results. Once we get a solid foundation of REPLENISHABLE ASINs, we can always go back and replace lower ROI ASINs with higher ones after we are making some predictable money.

P.A.T.H. - Prospect. Assess. Test. Harvest

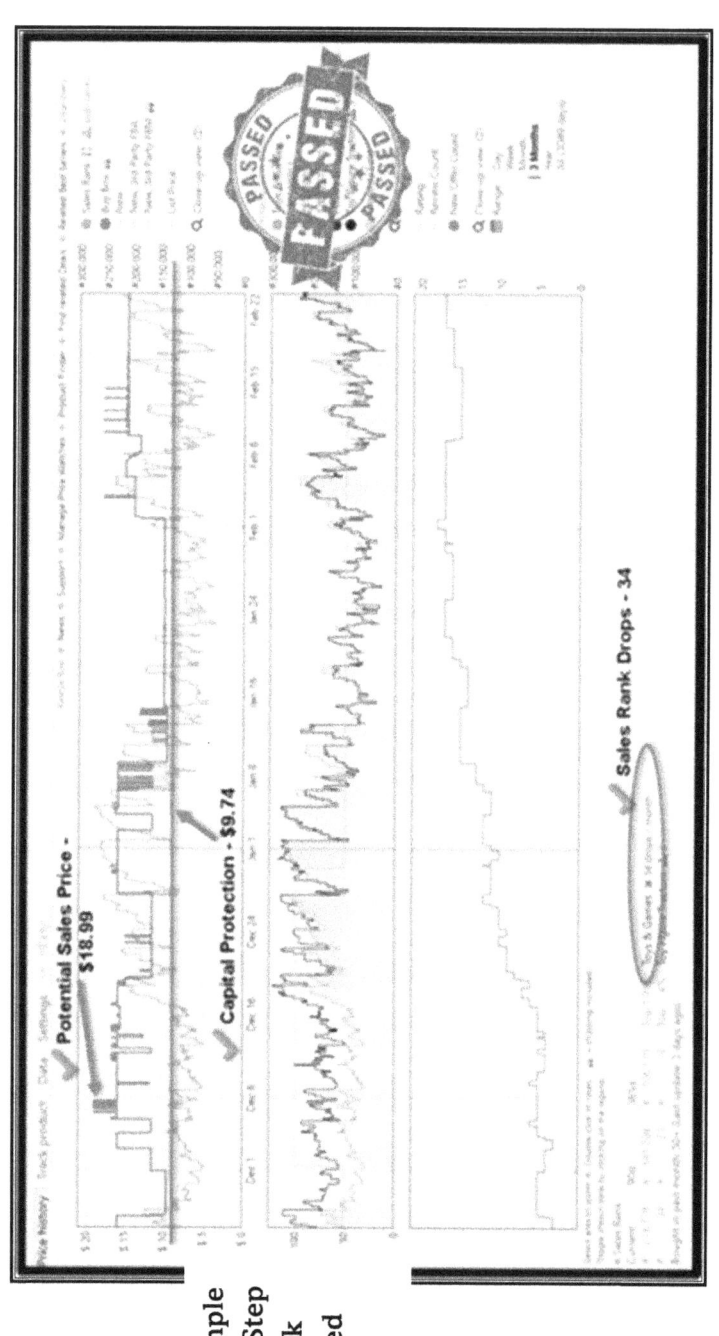

Example of 3-Step Check passed

Chapter 4: The Assessment Phase

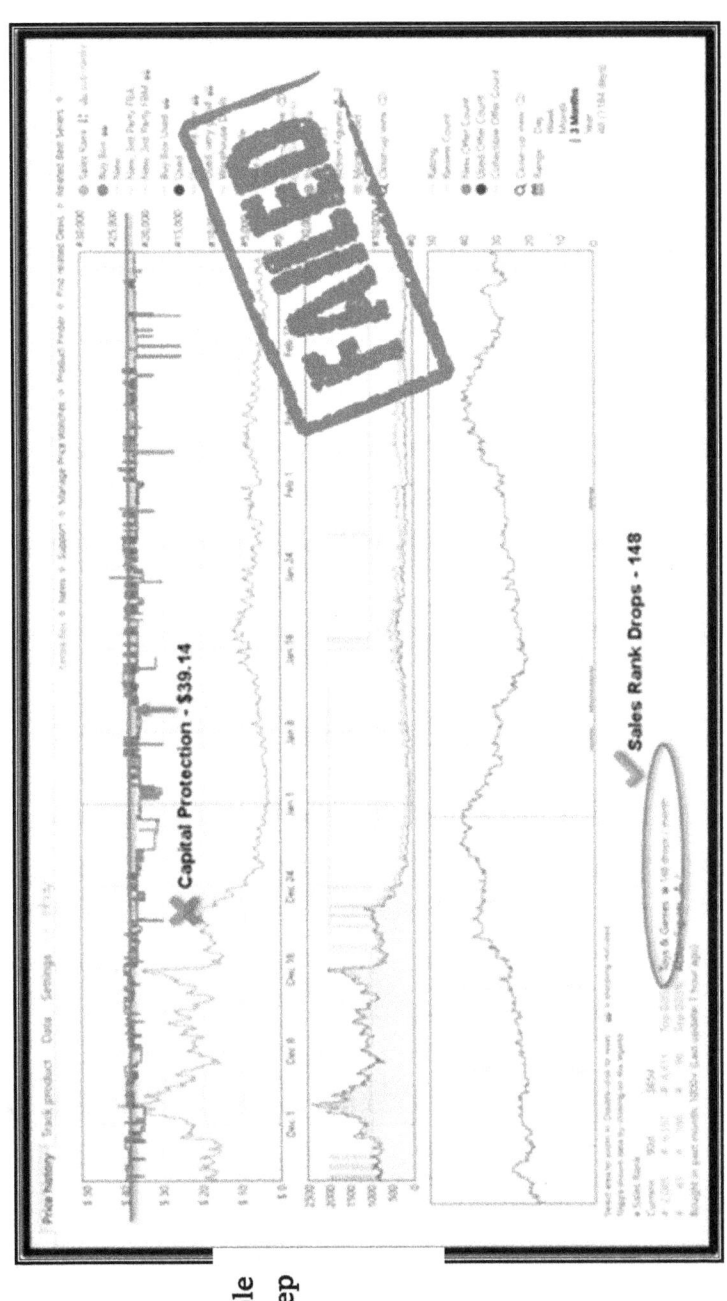

Example of 3-Step Check failed

P.A.T.H. - Prospect. Assess. Test. Harvest

The Framework in Action

Let's walk through how one of our recent workshop participants applied this framework to a real product evaluation. This Path to 100 ASINs graduate identified a promising skincare product and ran it through the **3-Step Check:**

For velocity, they observed 50 sales in the last 30 days – green light number one. For capital protection, they calculated their break-even at $18.75, well below the lowest sustained price in recent history of $24.99 – green light number two. For profit potential, their target price of $29.99 fell comfortably within the recent price range of $27.99 to $34.99 – green light number three.

With all three lights green, this accelerator program participant confidently ordered their test inventory. Notice they didn't need complex spreadsheets or years of experience – just three clear answers to three simple questions.

The Multi-Dimensional Buy Box: Your Secret Advantage

Here's a powerful insight about Amazon's Buy Box that regularly revolutionizes how our workshop participants think about pricing. Many sellers are surprised to learn that the same product can sell at different prices throughout the day and across different regions simultaneously. This concept, which we call the "multi-dimensional Buy Box," consistently transforms how our graduates approach their entire business strategy.

We've found this to be true in most retail situations – the same product often sells for different prices depending on when and where you're buying. Amazon's Buy Box works similarly. The price a customer sees can vary based on their location, available inventory in nearby warehouses, delivery speed options, and several other factors as well as the offer price, all impact the variability of the Buy Box.

One of our people we were working with, a former doubter who started with just a few hundred dollars, discovered this firsthand when she noticed she was making sales at $24.99 while other sellers were listing at $19.99. The reason? Her inventory happened to be closer to certain customers, making faster delivery possible. This discovery completely changed how she thought about pricing and competition.

Back-ordered Inventory

Let's take a quick look at How Amazon handles back-ordered items. Amazon's In-Stock Head start

Program is the reason we can see what items are back-ordered.

Selling Inventory that is on its way: Keeping Your Sales Flowing

Running out of stock on a hot-selling item is frustrating, but Amazon's In-Stock Head Start helps keep your sales going—even when inventory is temporarily unavailable.

Here's how it works: If Amazon predicts that your out-of-stock item will be replenished soon (based on your shipment history and tracking data as well as the available inventory for a listing), it may still be available for customers to buy with a delayed shipping date. This means your product remains discoverable in search results, and customers can place orders rather than moving on to a competitor.

Why does this matter? You can continue making sales, even before inventory arrives. It reduces the downtime between shipping inventory and fulfilling orders.

While this feature isn't guaranteed for every out-of-stock ASIN, it can help smooth out inventory gaps and keep your business running strong.

Chapter 4: The Assessment Phase

Using Amazon's In-Stock Head Start Program to our advantage

Now that we have a clearer understanding of the program, let's illustrate how it works with a simple, relatable story.

Imagine a bake sale where five bakers are selling brownies. Only one has fresh brownies ready for immediate purchase at $4.99. The other four are offering lower prices, ranging from $0.99 to $2.99, but there's a catch—they won't have brownies available for a few hours.

As customers approach, they're naturally curious about the lower prices, but the only baker with ready-to-eat brownies quickly sells out at full price—$4.99. Meanwhile, the bakers with the cheaper brownies don't make any immediate sales because their products aren't available yet.

This is exactly what happens when sellers enroll their products in the In-Stock Head Start Program but aggressively lower prices. They assume customers will always choose the lowest price, when in reality, availability often matters more than cost.

The first baker didn't try to compete on price. Instead, they waited until their brownies were

P.A.T.H. - Prospect. Assess. Test. Harvest

ready and sold them at a premium to customers who wanted them right away. The other bakers raced to the bottom on price, selling out before their product was even ready. By the time they could fulfill their orders, they had already locked themselves into lower profit margins and lost the chance to sell at a higher price when demand peaked.

The same thing happens on Amazon every day. Millions of shoppers end up paying less than they were willing to for products that take longer to arrive, simply because sellers—like you and me—failed to stock the right inventory in the right place at the right time.

As Jim Cockrum puts it:

"Today, millions of Amazon shoppers will pay LESS than they were willing to for items that will arrive SLOWER than they'd prefer, all because sellers LIKE YOU AND ME failed to stock the warehouse nearest the buyer with the most in-demand items being sold on Amazon."

Amazon's In-Stock Head Start program can sometimes lead to lower profits because products that are immediately available tend to get the sale, even at a higher price. Meanwhile, delayed inventory may struggle to compete, resulting in

Chapter 4: The Assessment Phase

missed sales or the need to lower prices to attract buyers before the stock becomes readily available.

P.A.T.H. - *Prospect. Assess. Test. Harvest*

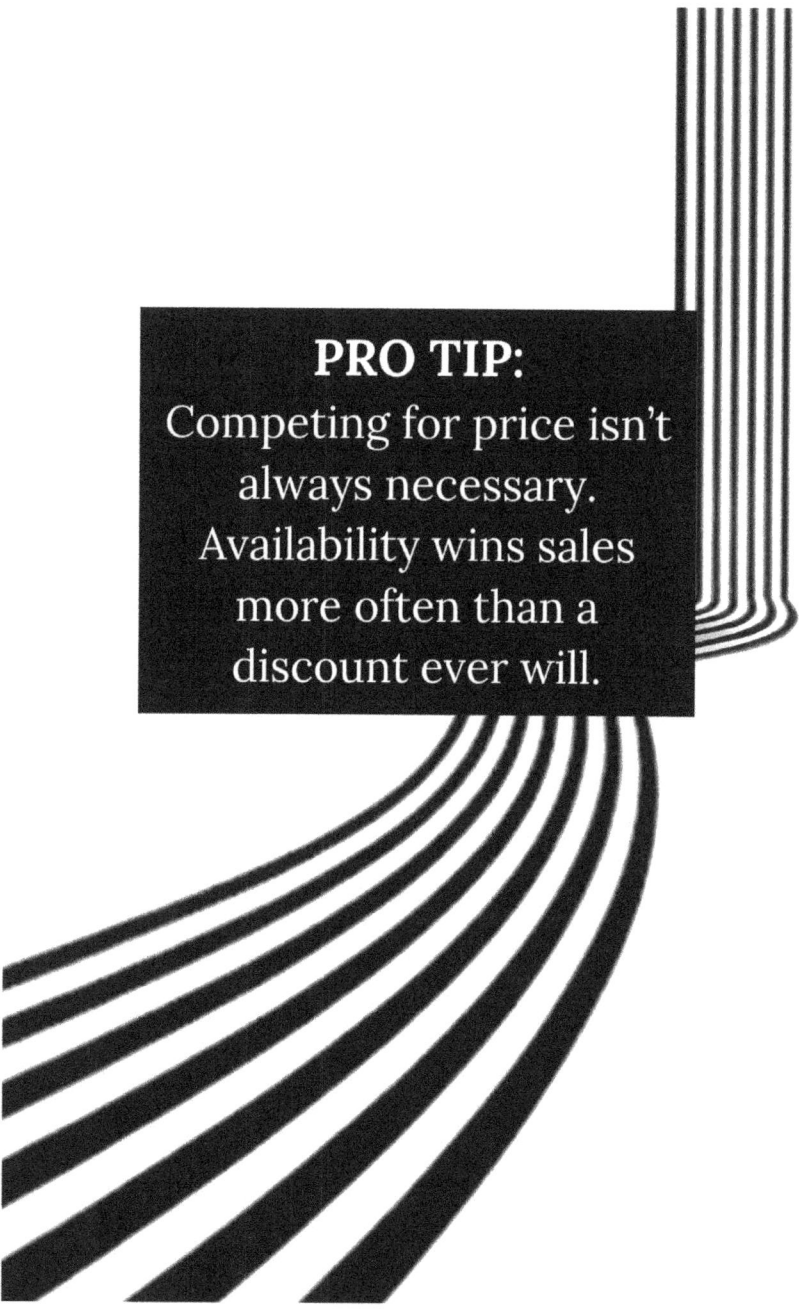

PRO TIP:
Competing for price isn't always necessary. Availability wins sales more often than a discount ever will.

Chapter 4: The Assessment Phase

The Hidden Benefits of Testing

At our live workshops, we often ask attendees an interesting question: "Would you be willing to work for 6-9 months without profit if it meant building a foundation for a predictable, sustainable, and scalable business?" The answer is almost always an enthusiastic "Yes! Of course!" Then we share the good news – you don't have to wait that long to see profits while building your foundation and establishing trust with Amazon.

Let me explain how this journey typically unfolds. In the beginning, you'll start by sending in test orders – just a few units of several different TESTABLE ASINs. Some of these tests will become what we call REPLENISHABLE ASINs (products you'll keep restocking), while others won't make the cut. But here's the exciting part: the more you test, the better your success rate becomes.

Have you ever planted a garden? First, you're just planting seeds (your test orders), not knowing which ones will thrive. But soon enough, you'll start seeing some sprouts – maybe your weekly shipment will include 5 new TESTABLE ASINs with a few units each, plus 3 REPLENISHABLE ASINs that you're restocking with 5-10 units each. Stay consistent with this pattern, sending in a few new tests each week, and something magical happens:

P.A.T.H. - Prospect. Assess. Test. Harvest

suddenly you'll find yourself shipping more replenishment inventory than test inventory.

This is when your profit curve starts to look like a hockey stick – after staying relatively flat during the testing-only phase, once you begin replenishing more ASINs than you are testing, it begins to curve sharply upward. While it might take several weeks to reach this turning point, once you do, the growth potential is limitless.

But here's what's really fascinating– the benefits go far beyond just profits. Every successful sale you make on Amazon, whether it's from a test product or a proven winner, builds your seller credentials in multiple ways:

- Your Account Health Rating improves with successful transactions

- You can collect valuable seller feedback from customers

- You gain hands-on experience with Amazon's platform

- Your sourcing skills get sharper with each product you evaluate

- Amazon gradually lifts brand and category restrictions as you prove yourself

Chapter 4: The Assessment Phase

Let us share something that surprises many new sellers: Amazon doesn't track or care about your profit margins. They don't know if you made any money or not. What matters to them is that you're providing a good customer experience and completing successful transactions. Every sale builds your credibility, regardless of whether that product becomes a long-term winner for you. This accumulated trust is what leads Amazon to automatically remove those brand and category restrictions a little at a time, as you build your track record.

Consider this example from one of our workshop participants. In their first month, they tested twenty products. While only two became long-term winners, the experience proved invaluable. Their Account Health Rating improved, they earned their first positive seller feedback, and – most importantly – they gained the confidence to make faster, better decisions about future products. Those eighteen "failed" tests? They weren't really failures at all – they were the steppingstones that helped build their foundation for success that came with plenty of added value.

Remember, many successful Amazon sellers started exactly where you are now – with test orders and a willingness to learn. The key is to view each test not just as a potential profit opportunity, but as an

P.A.T.H. - Prospect. Assess. Test. Harvest

investment in your business's foundation and your growth as a seller.

Your Essential Testing Tools

Just as a carpenter needs the right tools to build a house, you need the right tools to evaluate ASINs. But don't worry – your toolbox doesn't need to be complicated. You already know about Keepa, your market research assistant. You really don't need anything else. You can use Amazon's free revenue calculator to see the fees for any given listing. We find that a programmable on-page calculator, like AZ Insight or RevSeller can really speed the process along, but it is optional, and you can decide on that later.

One of our more successful students shared with us that starting simple is often the best approach. Instead of complicated spreadsheets or expensive software, he began with just a regular notebook, like a journal. On each page, he tracked one product, noting basic information like his checkpoint answers, how well the product sold, and what he learned along the way. The amazing part? Even though he now runs a mid-six figure business, he still follows this same straightforward approach. His story proves that you don't need fancy tools or complex systems to build a successful Amazon business - sometimes the simplest solution is the best one.

Taking Your First Steps

Are you ready to put this knowledge into action? Let me share the simplest way to start. Pick several VIABLE ASINs from your list. Run each one through the **3-Step Check** we've discussed. Choose one that passes all three assessments and start your first test. That's all there is to it.

Remember, you're not aiming for perfection – you're aiming for progress. Just as you wouldn't expect to build a house in a day, you don't need to master everything about testing immediately. Start with a few listings, learn from the experience, and build from there.

Looking Ahead

In the next chapter, we'll dive into the exciting part – actually running your tests. We'll talk about how many units to order, what pricing strategies work best, and exactly what to monitor during your test period. But for now, focus on mastering this **3-Step Check**. Practice evaluating ASINs using this framework until it becomes second nature.

P.A.T.H. - Prospect. Assess. Test. Harvest

Think about where you were when we started this chapter. Maybe you felt overwhelmed by all the decisions involved in testing products. Now you have a clear, simple framework to guide those decisions. The **3-Step Check** isn't just a tool – it's your path to confident action in building your Amazon business.

We love sharing this common success pattern from our accelerator program: a participant who initially couldn't make a single decision transformed their approach using the **3-Step Check**. In just their first week, they confidently tested five products. More importantly, within a few months, they had identified over a dozen REPLENISHABLE ASINs. This journey from paralysis to progress isn't unique - it's a path we've watched countless sellers follow, and it's available to you as well.

Ready to move on to testing? Let's keep building your to Amazon FBA success. In the next chapter, we'll show you exactly how to turn these TESTABLE ASINs into REPLENISHABLE ASINs which help you build a predictable, sustainable, scalable book of business.

Chapter 4: The Assessment Phase

CHAPTER 4
RESOURCES
and
IMPLEMENTATION
TOOLS

Chapter 4: The Assessment Phase

Resources and Implementation Tools

To help you put these concepts into action, we've prepared several resources available at OfficialOlsons.com/path

Essential Downloads:

✓ **4-Week Test**ing Timeline Template

✓ Additional Keepa Chart Analysis

Bonus Materials:

- Assessment criteria checklist
- Testing protocol videos

Next Steps:

1. Customize your testing timeline
2. Set up your pricing strategy
3. Create your assessment criteria
4. Plan your first product test

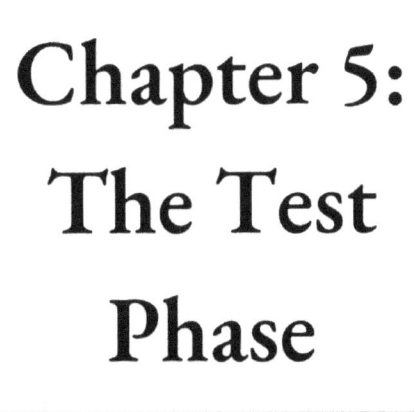

Chapter 5: The Test Phase

P.A.T.H. - Prospect. Assess. Test. Harvest

Chapter 5: The Test Phase

The 4-Week Test: Your Path to Confident Decisions

Do you remember your first day of school? That mixture of excitement and nervousness as you stepped into the classroom? That's exactly how many sellers feel when they're ready to start their first ASIN test. You've done your homework with the **Pre-Flight Inspection** to identify VIABLE ASINs, used the **3-Step Check** to determine TESTABLE opportunities, and now it's time for the moment of truth -- actually testing your chosen ASIN to see if it is a REPLENISHABLE ASIN.

Understanding the True Value of Testing

Before we dive into the testing process itself, we want to share something crucial that many sellers misunderstand: the real value of testing goes far beyond just finding REPLENISHABLE ASINs. Every test you run, regardless of its outcome, builds multiple forms of value for your business. After all, virtually every test results in a sale. Amazon doesn't know or care if you made money from that sale.

Chapter 5: The Test Phase

Amazon cares that you have had a successful transaction with one of its customers.

Think of testing not only as a validation tool, but also as an investment in your business infrastructure and building blocks of your business intelligence. With each test/sale, you're building your Amazon seller metrics, gaining valuable market insights, and developing pattern recognition skills that will serve you throughout your selling journey. It's like going to the gym -- every workout makes you stronger, whether or not you hit a new personal record that day.

Many of our workshop participants and coaching clients share a common initial mindset. They start their Amazon journey laser-focused on finding immediate winners, often paralyzed by the fear of making the "wrong" choice. One of our coaching program graduates perfectly illustrated this transformation. Like many beginners, they initially overlooked the valuable learning opportunities that come with each test, focusing solely on profit potential.

The breakthrough came when they understood our capital protection strategy - knowing they could recover their investment at minimum. This safety net transformed their approach to testing. Instead of fearing mistakes, they began actively seeking more products to test, recognizing that every transaction, whether it became a long-term winner or not, contributed to their success on Amazon.

This workshop participant discovered what we've seen time and again: even tests that don't meet minimum requirements for replenishment serve a valuable purpose. Each successful transaction builds trust with Amazon, improves seller metrics, and contributes to the lifting of restrictions (ungating) across more categories and brands. This understanding transforms testing from a scary proposition into an exciting opportunity for business growth.

In the beginning it feels like everything is a test - because it is. However, after you've tested a number of products and identified REPLENISHABLE ASINs, the script flips and you will have very few tests compared to replenishments.

The Psychology of Testing: Overcoming Analysis Paralysis

One of the biggest challenges new sellers face isn't technical – it's psychological. The fear of making a wrong decision can be paralyzing. We see this illustrated perfectly in our workshops, where participants often get stuck in what we call the "just a little longer" trap. One memorable example involves a participant who had been testing their first product for six months when they joined our program.

This seller's frustration was palpable as they described their situation: constantly waiting for the perfect moment to make a decision, always finding reasons to gather more data, perpetually deciding to wait "just a little longer." Their experience mirrors what we see so often - the endless cycle of seeking absolute certainty.

This pattern appears so frequently that it led us to develop our **4-Week Test** framework. Through working with hundreds of sellers, we've discovered this time frame provides the optimal balance: enough data to make informed decisions without falling into analysis paralysis. It's sort of like conducting a scientific experiment -- you need clear parameters and a defined endpoint to draw meaningful conclusions.

The Multi-Dimensional Nature of Amazon's Featured Price

One of the most powerful insights that can transform your testing strategy is understanding how Amazon's Featured Price really works. Most sellers assume they're always competing against the lowest price, but Amazon's pricing system is far more sophisticated and this creates hidden opportunities for higher profits during testing.

The Buy Box (or Featured Price) operates across multiple dimensions simultaneously. Let's explore each one and see how understanding them can give you a competitive edge.

Time of Sale Component

The same product can sell at different prices throughout the day. In fact that featured price is often moving up and down all day long. While Keepa charts typically show the lowest price for that day, each sale potentially occurs at a different price point, much like stock market prices. Our accelerator program graduates regularly share their amazement at discovering substantial Buy Box price fluctuations occurring within just one day of monitoring their listings.

A critical aspect of timing that many sellers overlook is Amazon's In-Stock Head Start Program. Earlier we mentioned how this strategy that Amazon uses to keep inventory available to purchase even when delivery will not be in 48 hours or less. Let's visit this concept again. This innovative program allows customers to find and purchase products that are temporarily out of stock but expected to be restocked soon. While this seems

Chapter 5: The Test Phase

straightforward, understanding its nuances gives savvy sellers a significant advantage.

Here's what most sellers miss: When inventory is purchasable by a customer as a result of the In-Stock Head Start program, it doesn't necessarily mean it's available to any customers within the standard 48-hour Prime delivery window. Let's call this time frame before the units are available to someone within 48-hours the positioning period. This period creates an interesting dynamic where sellers often react prematurely to perceived "slow sales" by lowering their prices. What they don't realize is that the slow sales might be due to delivery timing rather than pricing. We can use this to our advantage by starting our test only after we know we are not competing on time as well as price. The time issue will solve itself if we leave our inventory alone until it is no longer outside the 48-hour window.

What happens, you may ask, if I begin selling items before the units are within the 48-hour delivery window? Well, if you are selling those items at your highest price and getting sales even when time is an issue, the price is clearly not a problem. Some might even try raising their price if this happens. We'll discuss this more in the **4-Week Test** Journey section.

P.A.T.H. - *Prospect. Assess. Test. Harvest*

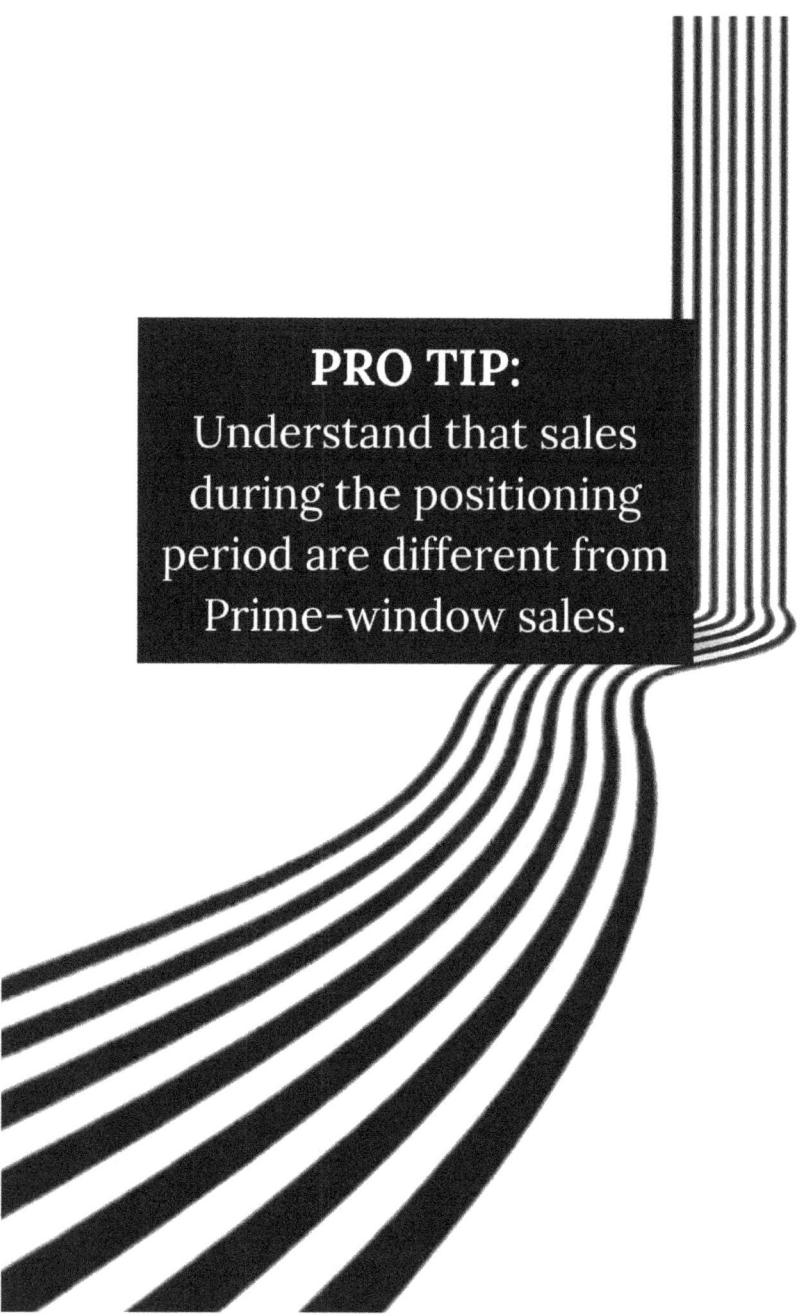

PRO TIP: Understand that sales during the positioning period are different from Prime-window sales.

Chapter 5: The Test Phase

This transformation in understanding inventory strategy occurs regularly in our accelerator program. They start to see that a frequent pattern emerges as new sellers see their inventory as purchasable but panic when sales don't immediately follow, often rushing to lower prices unnecessarily. This sometimes creates a needlessly low-price history. Through our training, they discover that real competition only begins once inventory is properly positioned for Prime delivery. By maintaining stable pricing during the positioning phase, our clients report consistently achieving higher margins.

Understanding Keepa's Limitations

While Keepa provides invaluable data for sellers, it's important to understand its limitations. Our program participants often discover they're making sales at prices higher than what Keepa shows as the Buy Box price. This revelation typically comes as a pleasant surprise during.

One of our workshop graduates shared compelling evidence of this phenomenon in a podcast interview. Their Seller Central reports showed multiple sales at prices significantly above what Keepa displayed as the Buy Box price for those same days. Here's the shocker: this is completely normal and happens consistently.

This disconnect between Keepa's data and actual sales occurs for several reasons. First, Keepa typically captures the lowest Buy Box price it encounters during its periodic checks but doesn't record every price change throughout the day. Second, regional price variations mean sellers might be winning Buy Box sales at higher prices in certain areas, even while lower prices exist elsewhere. Finally, the interaction between delivery speed, geography, and pricing creates opportunities that Keepa's data simply can't capture.

This insight reinforces the teaching of our clients to use Keepa as a guide rather than gospel (albeit, a highly trusted guide!). While it's an essential tool for initial research and trend analysis, actual sales often tell a more profitable story than what Keepa's charts suggest. This understanding helps our graduates maintain confidence in their pricing strategies, even when their prices appear higher than what Keepa reports as the Buy Box price.

Geography Component

Amazon's network of fulfillment centers creates natural regional disparities. When your inventory is physically closer to a customer than a competitor's stock, Amazon's algorithm often favors your offer -- even at a higher price point. This regional disparity

Chapter 5: The Test Phase

stems from Amazon's commitment to delivery speed.

One of our Path to 100 ASINs graduates demonstrated this concept perfectly with their kitchen gadget listing. Despite competitors dropping prices to $17.99, she maintained a $24.99 price point and continued making sales. The success stemmed from her inventory's proximity to high-demand regions, which created a delivery speed advantage. This positioning led Amazon's system to feature her higher-priced offer in certain regions, even though they weren't the lowest-priced seller.

P.A.T.H. - Prospect. Assess. Test. Harvest

Delivery Speed Component

This is where understanding customer behavior becomes crucial. Amazon has done a remarkable job training its customers to prioritize delivery speed over price. Prime members, in particular, often choose much higher-priced items that can arrive faster. Think about it -- Amazon's entire business model is built on convenience, not lowest prices. The same way we don't think much of paying twice as much for that bottle of water at a gas station because of the convenience, Amazon customers are willing to pay more to get faster delivery.

Chapter 5: The Test Phase

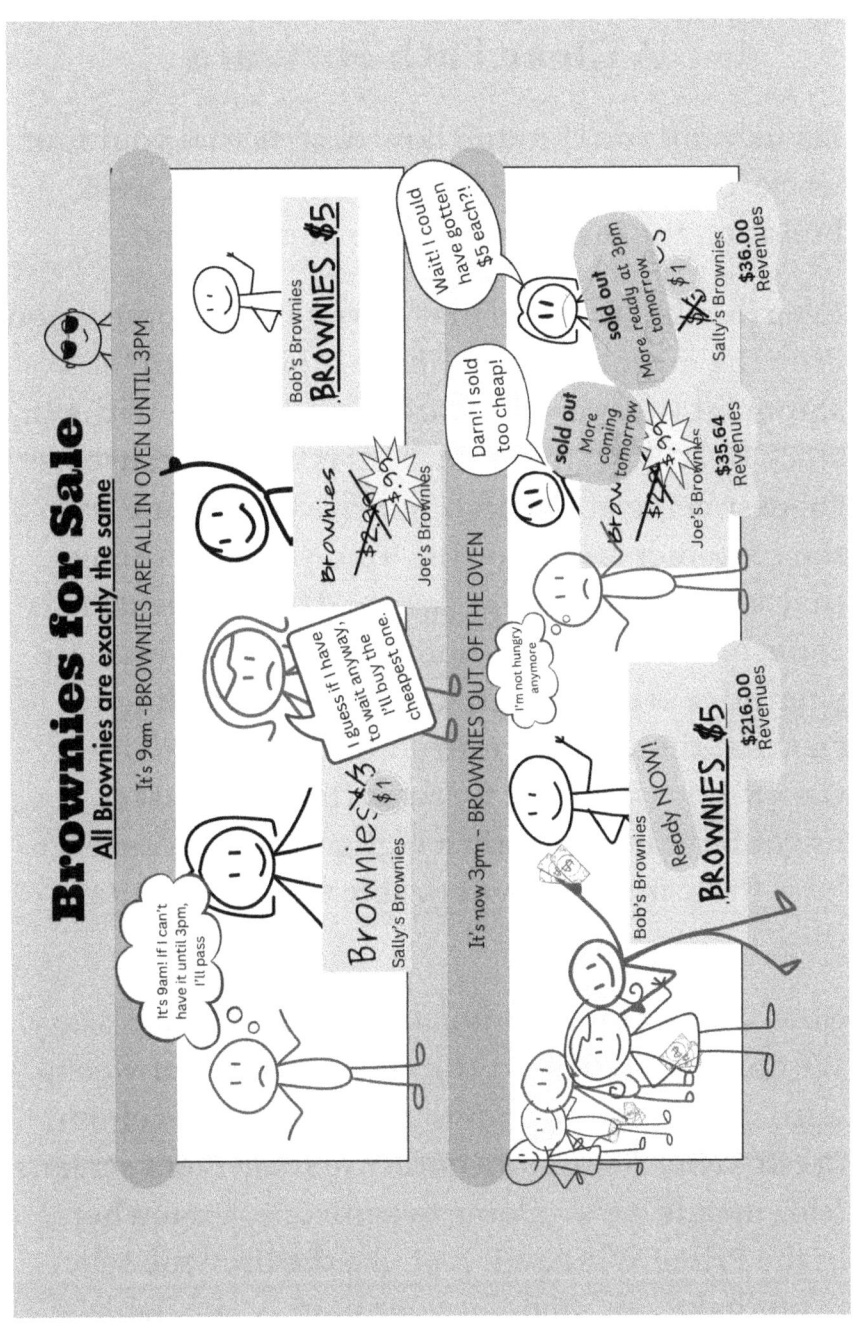

P.A.T.H. - Prospect. Assess. Test. Harvest

Your 4-Week Testing Journey: A Clear Path Forward

Let us walk you through how to structure your four weeks of testing. It's a journey where each week builds on the insights from the previous one.

Keep in mind that you may have sales as soon as you drop the inventory off (or have it picked up) for shipment to Amazon's warehouse because of the In-stock Head Start program. This is great because we suggest being at the highest price on day one and the customer is purchasing from you even though they won't receive it for several days or weeks. This could also be an indication that you could increase your price even further. If the listing is selling so fast that there is never inventory available within the 48-hour window, it seems this tiny market might be able to sustain a higher price. Because we have these insights, we are able to take advantage of this.

Now, we want to do a full **4-Week Test** if necessary. We don't want to start the clock on the four weeks until our inventory shows in the Available column in our Seller Central inventory management screen. (this means it's available to someone, somewhere, in the Prime Window). Just like the brownie sellers in our bake sale analogy, your item is "available"

Chapter 5: The Test Phase

when the brownies are actually on the table, not still being mixed or still in the oven. We don't want to begin adjusting our price until we know we have time handled. In other words, until we know a product is in the Prime Delivery window for a customer.

P.A.T.H. - *Prospect. Assess. Test. Harvest*

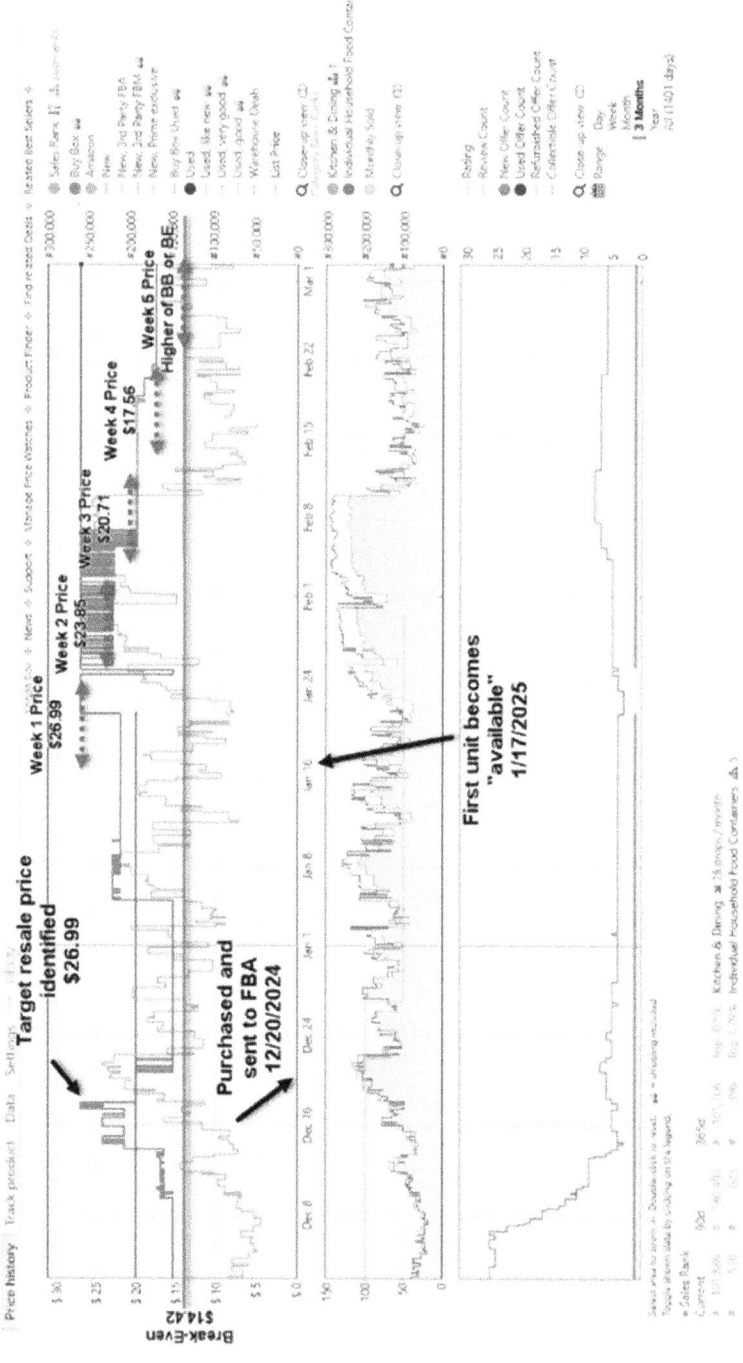

Chapter 5: The Test Phase

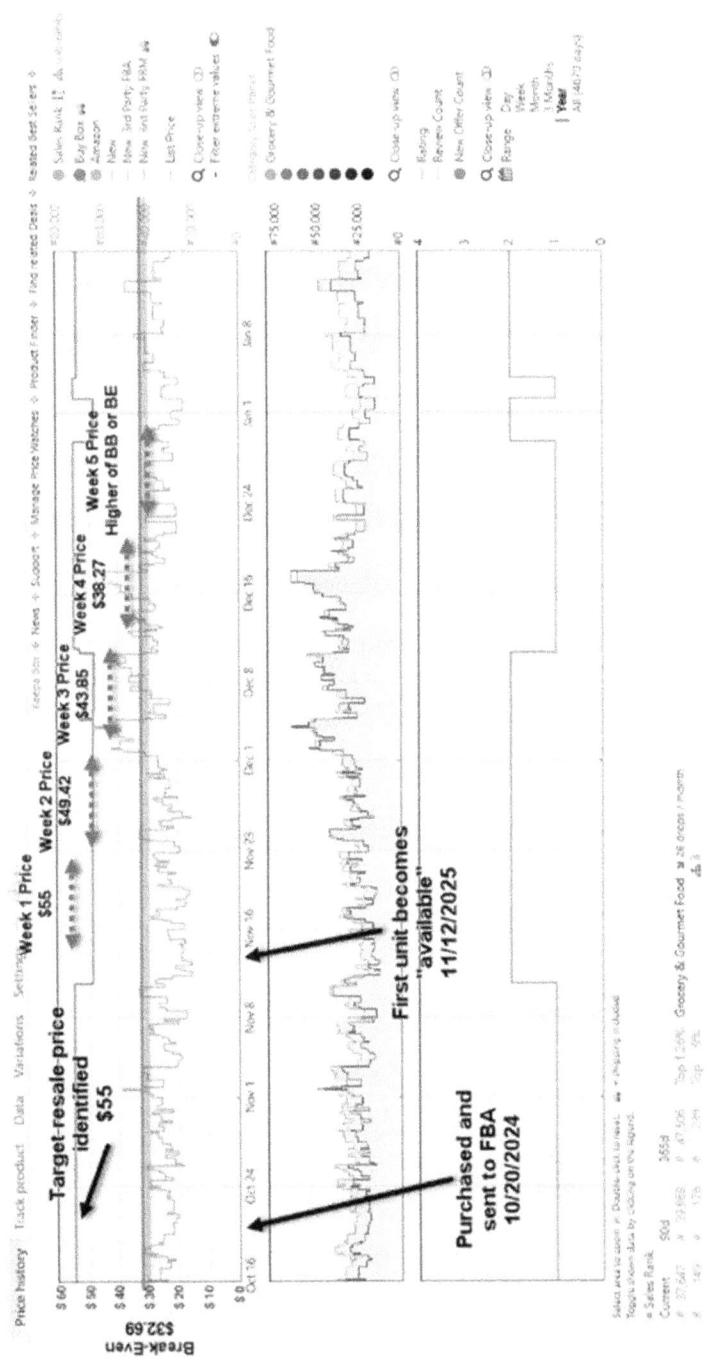

P.A.T.H. - Prospect. Assess. Test. Harvest

In your first week, you're introducing yourself to the market. Just like starting at a new school, you want to observe and learn before making any big moves. Your product may be purchasable, but it is not competitive from a delivery standpoint. If you make sales in your first week, you know this is a REPLENISHABLE ASIN and you can put it on your regular restock list. If you don't make a sale during this week, lower your price a little to see if a lower price will result in sales. Leaving each price point for a full week will not only be much easier to manage than many price changes during that time, it will also give enough time for a reasonable test at that price point.

During week two, if you haven't yet made a sale, you'll start fine-tuning your approach based on what you learned in week one. This is when you might make your first price adjustments. As with week one, at the end of week two if you have made sales, you have a REPLENISHABLE ASIN and you can put it on your restock list. If you have not made a sale, lower your price.

Week three is when patterns really start emerging. You'll begin to see how your inventory performs across different regions and times of day. This is when, one of our most successful sellers, realized that his highest-margin sales often came from regions where his inventory was positioned closest

Chapter 5: The Test Phase

to customers. We don't have any control over where Amazon places our inventory, but Amazon is very good at logistics, and we count on them to know where the inventory will do best. Again, if you have made sales, you have a REPLENISHABLE ASIN and you can put it on your restock list. If you have not made a sale, lower your price.

When you begin week four, you should price your offer at your lowest acceptable price. The lowest price it would make sense to replenish. This is the last chance to become a REPLENISHABLE ASIN. By the end of week four, you're ready to make your replenishment decision based on actual data rather than speculation. As our Path to 100 ASINs Workshop graduates have discovered, this structured approach provides both protection and insight - you're gathering crucial market intelligence while maintaining the ability to recover your investment.

If you have not made a sale by the end of week four, you have given it time to get to the warehouse and available to the customer within 48 hours and you have given it another month. You have enough information to make the decision, so make it. If you have not yet sold any, the decision is, that this is not currently a REPLENISHABLE ASIN. The ASIN is still a VIABLE ASIN and should go back on that list for potential future evaluation.

P.A.T.H. - Prospect. Assess. Test. Harvest

But wait! You still haven't made a sale! What, you may ask, do I do with the inventory I was testing? At this point, you should lower your price enough to get it sold. If you have done your homework, you won't usually have to go below your break-even price, and you will get all your money back. Don't hold out and spend money on storage fees and lower your Inventory Performance Index. Get your money back so you can put it into another chance for potential profit.

Chapter 5: The Test Phase

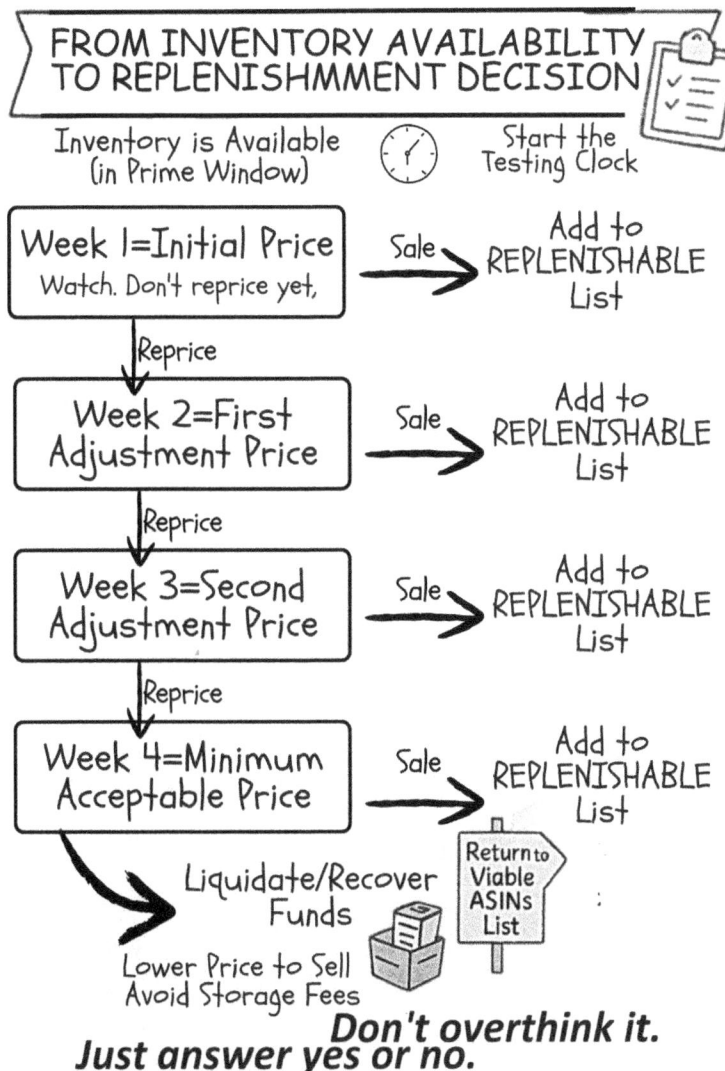

Test Quantity: Small Batches, Big Insights

When sellers ask me how many units they should test, we often use the car-buying analogy: you don't need to drive cross-country to know if a car is right for you. A well-planned test drive tells you everything you need to know. Similarly, testing 3-5 units gives you a great balance between gathering meaningful data and managing risk. Even 1-2 can be a good test if you are tight on capital.

The Four Price Points Strategy: Your Safety Net

Before starting each test, you need to establish four key price points that will guide your decision-making. Think of these as your guardrails – they keep you safely on track while giving you room to maneuver.

Your **Initial Price** is your highest justified price based on market data. It's like starting a negotiation – after the inventory is showing as available in your Seller Central inventory screen, you will start your **4-week test**ing clock. You should already be priced at the highest reasonable point and leave it there for a full week. You will have your **First Adjustment Price** if there is still no sale at the

Chapter 5: The Test Phase

beginning of week 2. This price will be about 1/3 of the way to your minimum acceptable price. If you still don't have a sale by the end of week 2, go to your **Second Adjustment Price** and leave it there for a week. If there is still no sale, you will go another 1/3 of the way to your minimum acceptable price. If you still have no sales after week 3, your next price adjustment is to your **Minimum Acceptable Price**. This is your floor for replenishment – if you can't make a sale at this price, the product isn't a good candidate for restocking. Finally, your **Liquidation Price** will likely protect your investment if things don't go as you had hoped.

P.A.T.H. - *Prospect. Assess. Test. Harvest*

Sample Pricing Strategy Table

Target Resale Price	Break-Even Resale Price	20% Resale Price	Profit Spread	Incremental Change Amount
$ 55.00	$ 32.69	$ 37.82	$ 17.18	$ 5.73
Week 1	$ 55.00			
Week 2	$ 49.27	} Replenish any items that sell during this period.		
Week 3	$ 43.55			
Week 4	$ 37.82			
Week 5	$ 32.69	Do not replenish		

Chapter 5: The Test Phase

Advanced Time-Based Competition Strategies

One seller's experience with a popular kitchen gadget shows the power of understanding time-based competition. During the positioning period, his competitors kept dropping their prices from $24.99 to $19.99 and so on, thinking they weren't competitive. He maintained his $24.99 price, knowing his inventory wasn't yet positioned for Prime delivery. Once it was properly positioned, he captured most of the sales at full price while his competitors had unnecessarily reduced their margins and sold at lower prices than they needed to.

Seasonal selling provides perfect examples of how understanding Amazon's systems leads to better profits. One of our mentoring clients observed a common pattern during back-to-school season: sellers would panic and drop prices by 15-20% simply because their inventory was not selling when it showed extended delivery times. However, by applying their knowledge of the positioning period, this seller maintained higher prices and ultimately captured better margins once their inventory was properly positioned for Prime delivery.

One of our accelerator program graduates discovered a powerful insight about Amazon's regional delivery system. He noticed that his inventory became available for Prime delivery in different regions at different times. Instead of immediately dropping prices to compete nationally, he maintained higher prices throughout the process. This strategy paid off because customers in areas where his products were Prime-eligible would purchase at the higher price point, simply because items could be delivered quickly. By keeping his prices steady, rather than racing to the bottom as soon as some of his inventory became available, he maintained better profits across all regions as his inventory gradually became Prime-eligible throughout the country.

Making Your Final Decision

By week four, you'll have gathered enough data to make a confident replenishment decision. We consistently remind our mentoring clients that early tests deliver value beyond just profits. Even when products just break even, sellers gain improved Account Health metrics, positive feedback, and invaluable market experience. We've watched countless participants transform these early learning experiences into remarkable success, often achieving 90%

Chapter 5: The Test Phase

test success rates within their first two months of applying these insights.

Looking Ahead

As you prepare to start testing, remember that many successful Amazon sellers started exactly where you are -- with one product and a willingness to learn. The **4-Week Test** system provides you with clear parameters for making confident decisions while building valuable business assets regardless of the outcome.

In our next chapter, we'll explore how to take your successful test results and build them into a sustainable, profitable part of your business. But for now, focus on mastering this testing process and appreciating the multiple forms of value each test creates for your business.

Ready to take the next step on your Amazon FBA success? Let's turn those REPLENISHABLE ASINs into the foundation of your thriving Amazon business.

CHAPTER 5
RESOURCES
and
IMPLEMENTATION
TOOLS

Chapter 5: The Test Phase

Resources And Implementation Tools

To help you put these concepts into action, we've prepared several resources available at

OfficialOlsons.com/path

Essential Downloads:

✓ Additional **4-Week Test** Examples

Bonus Materials:

- Test results analysis guide

Next Steps:

1. Set up your tracking system

2. Define your profit targets

3. Create your testing schedule

4. Implement your first test

Chapter 6: The Harvest Phase

Chapter 6: The Harvest Phase

Reaping the Rewards of Successful Selling

Picture this: You've done the hard work of prospecting for VIABLE ASINs, assessing which ones are TESTABLE ASINs, and running your initial tests to see which are REPLENISHABLE ASINs. You've narrowed down a large list of TESTABLE ASINs to a select group of REPLENISHABLE ASINs and you now have proof that they sell consistently and profitably (for now) on Amazon. Now it's time for the fun part - harvesting the fruits of your labor and watching your business grow.

In the **Harvest Phase**, your focus shifts to replenishing your inventory of proven winners and scaling your operation. Just like a farmer tending their crops, you'll nurture your product "plants" - giving them the attention and resources they need to flourish. And as your "farm" matures, you'll enjoy the satisfaction and financial rewards of a thriving Amazon business.

Chapter 6: The Harvest Phase

The Replenishment Cycle

Think back to our farming analogy from the previous section. If the Prospecting Phase is surveying the land for fertile soil, the **Assessment Phase** is analyzing that soil's potential, and the Testing Phase is planting a variety of seeds to see what takes root, then the **Harvest Phase** is collecting the produce from your top-performing "plants" and continually re-sowing them.

In concrete terms, replenishing means restocking your inventory of profitable, fast-moving ASINs that you've thoroughly vetted. These are the listings that have proven themselves during the Testing Phase - the ones that reliably sell through and generate steady returns.

Your goal is to establish a regular replenishment cycle, systematically reordering your best ASINs so you maintain healthy stock levels and avoid running out (while balancing this with being overstocked). Over time, as you dial in your reordering cadence and quantities, you'll be able to largely automate this process, transforming your initial hustle into a well-oiled machine.

P.A.T.H. - Prospect. Assess. Test. Harvest

Evaluating Replenishables

Not every listing that makes it through the Testing Phase will remain a REPLENISHABLE ASIN in your business consistently. To determine which ASINs are worth the continued investment, you'll need to regularly evaluate your catalog against some key criteria:

Profit Margins - Are you consistently hitting your target profit per unit after all costs (product cost, shipping, Amazon fees, etc.)? Avoid getting emotionally attached to products; if an item isn't meeting your margin goals, it may be time to cut it loose and allocate that capital elsewhere, at least for now.

Sales Velocity - How quickly is the product turning over? Faster sell-through means a shorter cash conversion cycle and a higher ROI. Slower moving items tie up your money and may not be worth the opportunity cost.

Stability of Demand - Are sales steady and predictable or are they vulnerable to seasonality and demand shocks? More stable, evergreen products (think toothpaste, socks, kitchen supplies) tend to make better REPLENISHABLE ASINs than highly trendy or seasonal ones.

Chapter 6: The Harvest Phase

Expanding Your Farm

No matter how promising or profitable an ASIN might seem in the moment, the reality is that any listing's practicality can change in an instant due to factors beyond our control as sellers. For example:

- The brand owner might discontinue the product entirely, causing supply to evaporate.

- Amazon itself could start selling the item directly, squeezing out third-party sellers with their pricing power and/or reseller restrictions.

- Consumer tastes and demands can simply shift, cooling off interest in a once-hot product.

The key takeaway here is that change is a constant in the world of ecommerce. What's working brilliantly for our business today might be a dead-end tomorrow. So, relying too heavily on any single listing or even product category can unnecessarily increase your risk.

P.A.T.H. - Prospect. Assess. Test. Harvest

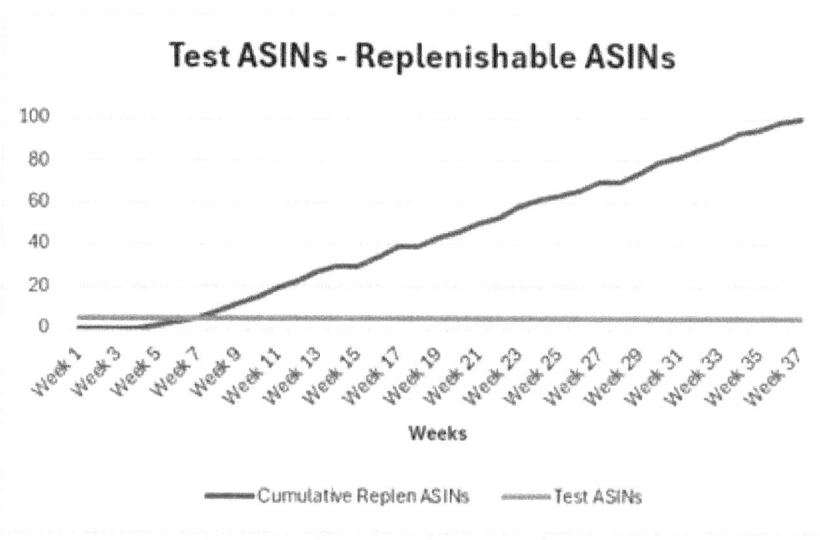

Chapter 6: The Harvest Phase

That's precisely why the most resilient, adaptable Amazon reselling businesses make a habit of always seeking out and testing new product opportunities as a form of continuous improvement even as they harvest profits from their established winners. No matter how much we scale up and systematize our operation, we must never stop prospecting for new ASINs to add to our catalog.

In fact, this need for continuous product innovation isn't unique to Amazon sellers - it's a core principle for essentially all retailers. Brick and mortar stores, for instance, are always cycling new products onto their shelves and retiring old ones to keep their assortment fresh and enticing for shoppers. And big consumer brands are forever tweaking their product lineups to capitalize on emerging trends and phase out fading ones.

Just as a farmer wouldn't plant identical crops on the same plot of land year after year (which would totally deplete the soil), we can't just keep selling the exact same set of products indefinitely and expect to thrive. We must regularly "rotate" new ASINs into our mix to keep our product selection vibrant, diverse, and resilient to disruptions.

Think of it this way: ASINs are like the nutrients that sustain our Amazon business. And our catalog is like the soil in which they grow. Over time, as market conditions evolve, certain ASINs will inevitably get "used up" and lose their potency - maybe a competitor swoops in and drives down profitability, maybe consumer interest wanes, maybe the manufacturer jacks up the price on us.

Chapter 6: The Harvest Phase

ROTATE YOUR CROPS, GROW YOUR CATALOG

WHY PRODUCT SCOUTING NEVER STOPS

P.A.T.H. - Prospect. Assess. Test. Harvest

Whatever the cause, those depleted ASINs stop delivering the "nutrients" (spendable profits) our business needs to grow and flourish. And if we haven't been steadily cultivating new ASINs to take their place, our once fertile catalog can quickly become barren and incapable of supporting us.

So just like a farmer, we must take the long view. We have to be strategic and proactive about replenishing our "soil" - our catalog - by constantly scouting for fresh "crops" to plant and test them for profitability. That way, by the time an existing ASIN has run its course and it's time to harvest our last profits from it, we've already got the next generation of products entering our pipeline, ready to take its place in the profit-producing rotation.

This discipline of unending product prospecting and introducing new TESTABLE ASINs every week is really the key to sustainable success as an Amazon seller. It protects us against over-reliance on any single ASIN, brand or product line, ensuring that our income streams stay diversified. It positions us to adapt nimbly as market trends shift, hopping on new opportunities while they are productive. And it equips us to play the long game, building a sustainable business that can thrive in any season.

So, in summary, expanding your ASIN "farm" through rigorous product scouting and thoughtful

Chapter 6: The Harvest Phase

catalog curation isn't just a smart strategy - it's an absolute necessity for any seller serious about building a predictable, sustainable, scalable Amazon business. A stagnant, undiversified product assortment is a dangerously vulnerable one in the quick-shifting world of ecommerce. But an agile, ever-evolving, intelligently rotating catalog? That's the foundation of a truly resilient book of business, one that's durable enough to sustain you for the long haul.

Applying the Pareto Principle

The Pareto Principle, commonly known as the 80/20 rule, manifests clearly in Amazon reselling businesses. Typically, about 20% of your ASINs will generate 80% of your profits, while the remaining 80% of your catalog contributes only 20% of your earnings. This isn't a flaw in your business model - it's a natural economic principle that appears across many industries and applications. Understanding and leveraging this principle can help you optimize your inventory investments and focus your energy where it matters most.

However, this principle shouldn't lead you to immediately slash your catalog down to just your top performers. Instead, use it as a lens to understand your business' dynamics and guide your growth strategy. Your "bottom 80%" serves several

P.A.T.H. - Prospect. Assess. Test. Harvest

crucial purposes: it provides diversification against market changes, offers opportunities to discover breakout products, and helps maintain a robust, resilient business model. More importantly, today's top 20% won't necessarily be tomorrow's winners. Market conditions change, competition emerges, and consumer preferences shift, making it essential to constantly feed new products into your pipeline.

This is why successful Amazon sellers maintain a steady rhythm of product prospecting and testing, even when their current catalog is performing well. By continuously introducing new ASINs into the mix, you're not just replacing underperformers - you're actively building the next generation of top performers. It's similar to cultivating a garden: while you're harvesting mature plants, you need to be simultaneously planting new seeds and nurturing younger plants to ensure continuous, sustainable growth. This approach ensures that as some products naturally decline in profitability, you already have new winners ready to take their place in your top 20%.

Chapter 6: The Harvest Phase

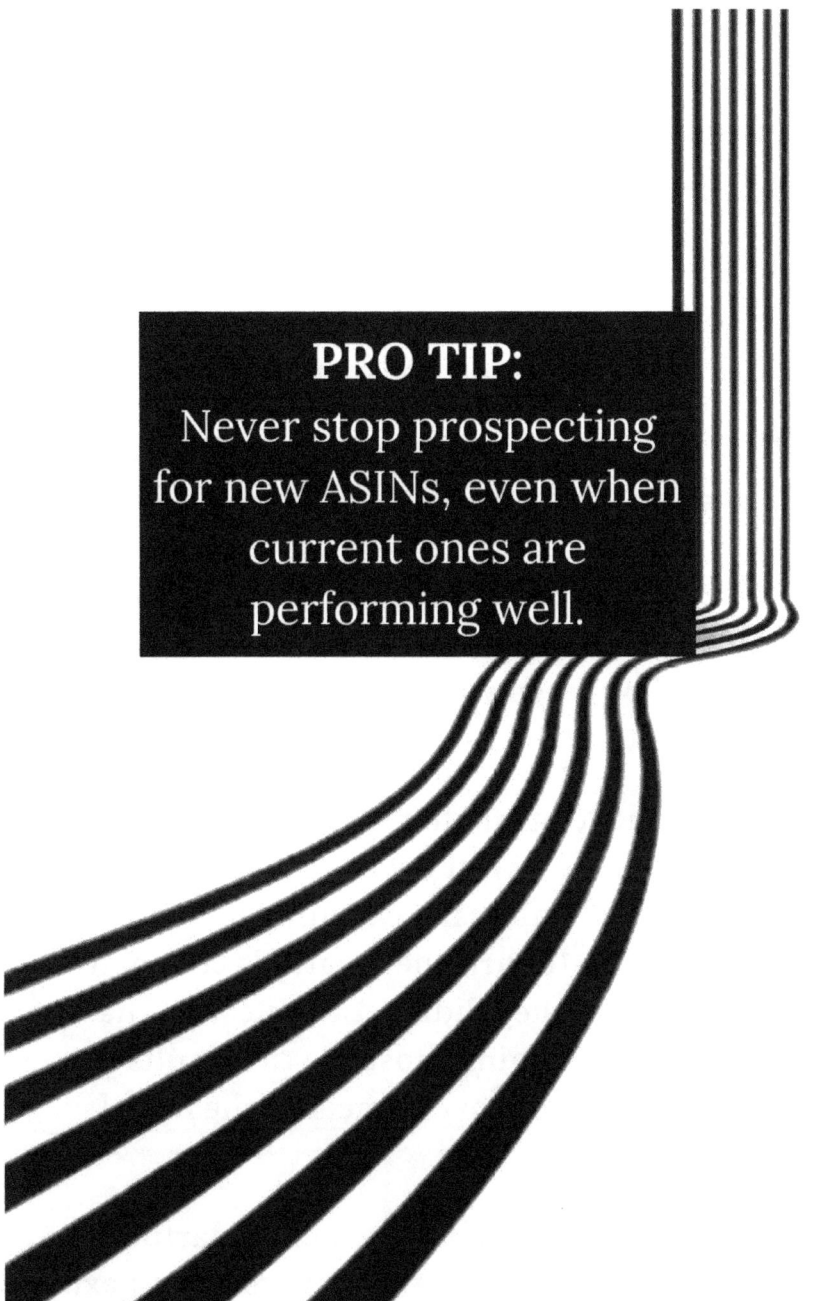

PRO TIP:
Never stop prospecting for new ASINs, even when current ones are performing well.

P.A.T.H. - Prospect. Assess. Test. Harvest

Pushing Up the Profitability Bar (Gradually!)

As you start to gain some traction and see more consistent returns from your Amazon business, it's natural to want to raise your standards for what constitutes a REPLENISHABLE ASIN. After all, why keep settling for slim margins and sluggish turnover when you could be aiming higher, right?

Well, not so fast. Let's remember that in your early days as a seller, you were probably thrilled to lock in a 20% ROI and 4 turns per year on a particular product. At that stage, any profitable, reliably selling ASIN felt like a major win! And that's exactly as it should be when you're just starting to build your foundation.

You see, while it's true that many experienced powerhouse sellers won't even consider an ASIN "replenishable" unless it's churning out at least a 50% ROI and 12-16 turns per year, it's crucial to understand that they didn't start out with that kind of velocity and margin. Those are the results of gradually leveling up over time, not the initial benchmark.

Think of your Amazon business like a dartboard. When you're first learning to play, you don't expect to be nailing bulls eyes right out of the gate. You're

Chapter 6: The Harvest Phase

excited just to hit the board consistently! Over time, as you hone your technique and develop your skills, you start to cluster more of your throws in the middle rings. And eventually, with tons of practice and refinement, you're able to concentrate your darts on that coveted bulls eye or consistently hit that triple-20 or double-17 when you need it.

P.A.T.H. - Prospect. Assess. Test. Harvest

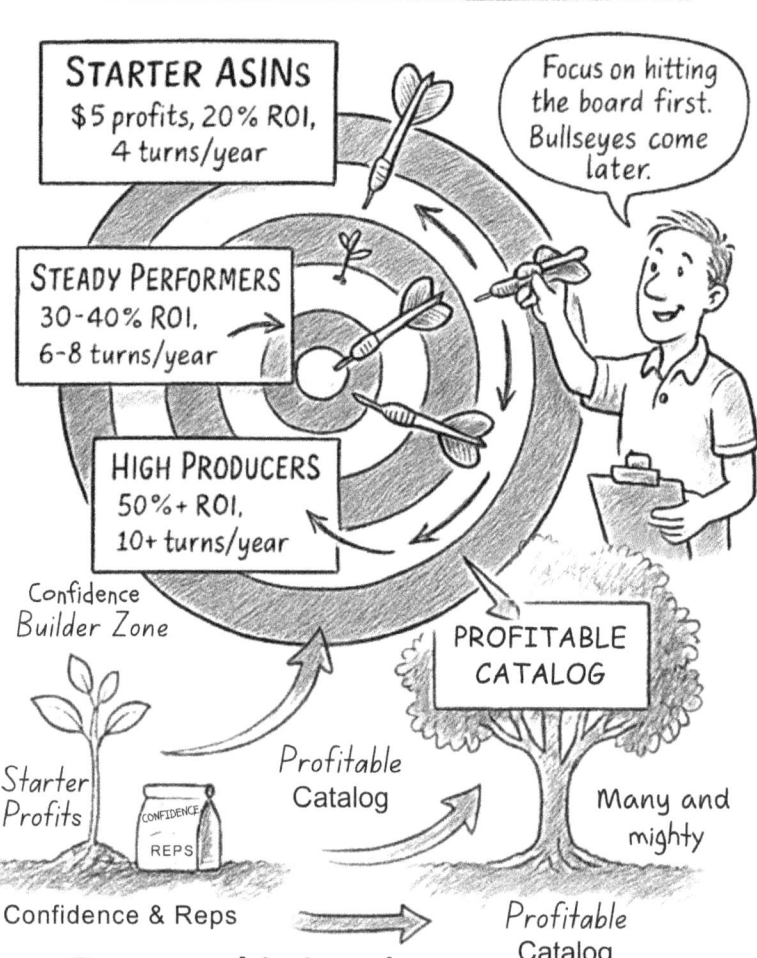

Focus on hitting the board first. Bullseyes come later.

Chapter 6: The Harvest Phase

Your profitability targets are like those rings on the dartboard. Hitting the outer ones is a necessary step to reaching the inner ones. You've got to build up to the center through repeated rounds of trial, error, and recalibration.

So, in your first months or even year as a seller, focus on cementing a core selection of ASINs that deliver reliable (if modest) profits and proven demand. Don't get caught up with chasing home runs when you're just learning to swing the bat! Those base hits (even bunts!) are crucial for growing your capital, fine-tuning your systems, and gaining the experience to gradually up-level.

Then, as you start to accumulate more sales history and build up some real buying power, you can progressively sharpen your criteria for what makes it into your REPLENISHABLE ASIN bucket. Slowly weed out the lower margin, slower turning products in favor of ASINs with beefier profit potential. Many veteran sellers find that a 50% ROI and 8-12 annual turns is a worthy benchmark for a sustainable REPLENISHABLE ASIN, after they have a foundation built.

Now, we know it might seem counter-intuitive to narrow your product focus like this, but here's the magic - it can actually speed up your overall growth! By ruthlessly zeroing in on your top

P.A.T.H. - Prospect. Assess. Test. Harvest

producers and cutting loose the dead weight, you'll be able to capture more profits to reinvest into new TESTABLE ASINs that are continually improving your book of business.

It's a powerful and positive feedback loop: Stronger products lead to bigger profits, which can fuel sharper product selection, which promotes still stronger products and even bigger profits! With each cycle, you nudge up your margins, fortify your market position, and set yourself up to climb to the next rung.

Just remember, this is a process of gradual refinement, not an overnight transformation. You've got to build the core foundation of your business before you can start chiseling away at it. We're talking about incremental gains here, single digit percentage increases. It may seem small but by increasing our gross profit percentage 1-2% each month, we can add 3%, 5%, 7% or more to the net profit numbers over the course of a year.

In the beginning, your priority should be to gain confidence, rack up reps, and build up your purchasing capital - even if the ASINs driving it are a bit skinnier than you'd like. View those initial profits as the fertilizer that will eventually grow your all-star ASIN orchard. Don't turn your nose up at a $5 bill just because it's not a $20 bill. Small

Chapter 6: The Harvest Phase

profits several times a month add up to significant gains.

Then, once you've put some real roots down and proven to yourself that you can source winners consistently, start turning up the dial. Prune out the ASINs that can't keep up with your rising standards and pour more of your growing capital into higher performing ASINs. Slowly but surely, sharpen your sights from the outer rings of the dartboard to the higher-scoring center.

It's important to remember that this is a journey, not a destination. No matter how much you'd like to, if you limit yourself to never taking anything less than a high standard, you will leave a lot of profits on the table and your business will grow very slowly. Trust the process, stay patient, and keep taking the next right step. With consistent positive actions over time, you'll look up one day and find yourself throwing bulls eyes virtually on-demand.

P.A.T.H. - *Prospect. Assess. Test. Harvest*

PRO TIP:
Start with modest profit goals and gradually increase your standards as your business grows.

Chapter 6: The Harvest Phase

Real World Examples of Perennial Refreshing

The imperative to continually refine and refresh your offers applies well beyond Amazon. Businesses in every industry must develop their book of products and services to keep pace with changing customer demands. Consider a few prime examples:

Skittles - Originally just fruit-flavored chewy candies, the Skittles brand has continually expanded its product line over the years to stay relevant to changing consumer tastes. From Sour and Wild Berry variations to Skittles Gum and even Skittles Yogurt, the brand has refused to rest on its signature product.

Dollar Shave Club - Famously launching with a subscription model for inexpensive basic razors, DSC has drastically expanded its product catalog to stay ahead of encroaching competition. Today, members can get everything from skincare products to deodorant to toothpaste delivered monthly, positioning DSC as a one-stop shop for men's grooming needs.

Netflix - Remember when Netflix started as a mail-order DVD rental service? As streaming video technology emerged, Netflix cannibalized its own core business to become a streaming pioneer. Now, it's even shifted to producing its own original content to differentiate itself from aggressive new competitors like Disney+ and Hulu. While their goal of streaming movies over the internet was not realistic in the early days of building the business, they knew where they were going and built their long-term strategic plan right into the company name: *Netflix*.

Just like these nimble brands, your Amazon business must embrace change to be sustainable. No ASIN lasts forever, so never stop exploring new VIABLE ASINs and TESTABLE ASINs to find REPLENISHABLE ASINs and adapting your core catalog.

Chapter 6: The Harvest Phase

> **PRO TIP:**
> When your business is cranking out consistently solid profits, you can now trade dollars for time instead of time for dollars. Now you can work from anywhere and start to live the dreams that motivated you to start your ecommerce adventure in the first place.

P.A.T.H. - Prospect. Assess. Test. Harvest

Systematizing for Scale

Of course, amidst all this talk of expansion and experimentation, it's crucial not to neglect the day-to-day execution of your core replenishment cycle. To achieve meaningful scale and liberate yourself from constant do-it-all hustle, you must build robust systems for restocking, monitoring, and overall business management.

This systematization starts with standardization and documentation of your core processes. Anything you find yourself doing more than a couple of times should be mapped out into a repeatable Standard Operating Procedure (SOP) that anyone on your team could follow, and should be continually updated as your business evolves.

This will free you up for high-level growth tasks like product strategy, developing key partnerships, and financial planning. In other words, for your business to reach its full potential, you need to spend more time steering the ship than shoveling coal in the engine room. Get to the point where you're working more ON your business than IN your business.

Ultimately, your goal should be a business that largely runs itself - where the replenishment of proven winners happens like clockwork, new

Chapter 6: The Harvest Phase

product prospects are perpetually bubbling up through your pipeline, and your daily involvement is minimal.

CHAPTER 6
RESOURCES
and
IMPLEMENTATION TOOLS

Chapter 6: The Harvest Phase

Resources And Implementation Tools

To help you put these concepts into action, we've prepared several resources available at OfficialOlsons.com/path

Essential Downloads:

✓ Business Scaling Roadmap

✓ FBA Business Operations Manual w/Standard Operating Procedures (SOP) Templates

Next Steps:

1. Customize your scaling roadmap

2. Implement your first SOP

3. Set growth milestones

4. Plan your scaling timeline

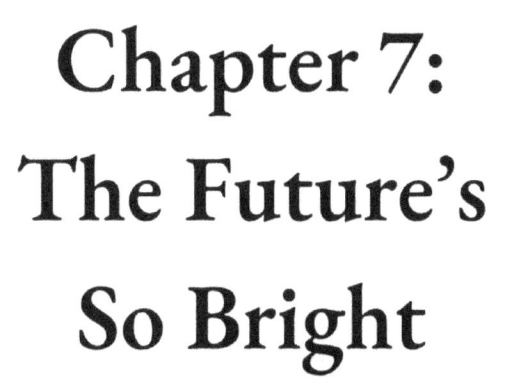

Chapter 7:
The Future's
So Bright

P.A.T.H. - Prospect. Assess. Test. Harvest

Chapter 7: The Future's So Bright

Enjoying the Harvest (and Tending Your Farm)

Take a moment to step back and appreciate the journey you've been on so far. Building a thriving, resilient Amazon business is no small feat - it's a winding path full of learning curves, trial and error, and sheer grit.

You saw an opportunity and seized it. You've leveraged fundamental frameworks to build a predictable, sustainable and scalable book of business. You dove headfirst into a completely unknown world of product research and system building, soaking up hard-earned lessons along the way. You weathered the Testing Phase, and trusted the process even when results were mixed.

And now, all those late nights and early mornings are starting to pay off - you're the proud owner of a real, profit-generating business with room to grow. That's huge! Pat yourself on the back and savor your accomplishment.

But as you know by now, the work of an Amazon seller is an ongoing journey. Even as you transition

Chapter 7: The Future's So Bright

into harvesting mode and start to see more consistent returns, it's crucial to keep tending to the fundamentals of your business because here's the thing - until you've established a solid baseline of steady sales across a diverse mix of products, your operation is still vulnerable. Fortunately, you have documented your processes and procedures so that you can hire others to do these tasks for you.

Think about it this way - if you're only juggling a small handful of ASINs, any little hiccup with one of them can send your whole system into a tailspin. When your catalog is thin, even minor disruptions can trigger major headaches.

That's why your first priority is to keep adding new VIABLE, TESTABLE and REPLENISHABLE ASINs to your catalog. Stay dogged about identifying and testing new product opportunities to mix in with your existing winners. The goal is to develop the stability that comes with a wide and varied assortment - so that if any one ASIN goes sideways, you can maintain stability.

Reliability, sustainability and scalability come from the relentless pursuit of diversification and depth. You're shooting for an expansive, and diverse catalog that is like a forest that provides strength, warmth and shelter for its inhabitants- not a handful of flimsy seedlings that topple in the first storm of the season. Your commitment to stick with the unglamorous work of laying the groundwork, even when the payoff feels slow will result in the sturdiest base.

Now, does that mean you have to wait until everything is perfect to start expanding and optimizing? Not at all! In fact, one of the most exciting parts of reaching this stage is that with a bit of a cushion beneath you, you can finally start to get strategic about up-level opportunities.

You see, once you've got a certain mass of steady-performing ASINs (AKA a foundational book of business), you leverage some serious power - the power to drive big results from relatively small tweaks. It's like the rudder on a boat. The more momentum the boat has, the less force it takes to steer it in a bold new direction.

That's the real magic of reaching critical mass with your book of business. You're no longer starting from scratch or grinding for every penny. With a diverse, stable foundation solidly in place, you gain the freedom to experiment with all kinds of levers for growth - levers that just weren't accessible (or worth pulling) when you were still scrambling to find your footing.

Chapter 7: The Future's So Bright

PRO TIP:
Diversification is key - build a forest of ASINs, not just a handful of trees.

P.A.T.H. - Prospect. Assess. Test. Harvest

Of course, that doesn't mean you can just "set it and forget it" once you've hit your stride. The world of ecommerce (and Amazon in particular) is always evolving. Customer trends, platform policies, supply chain dynamics - they're all shifting constantly, in ways both big and small. This is true in any business.

To stay nimble and protect your progress, you'll need to keep a vigilant eye on the horizon and be ready to pivot when necessary. Sometimes, like the Borg in Star Trek, you'll need to quickly adapt and re-calibrate in the face of new challenges or roadblocks (ask us how we know! ;). The more you can stay responsive to change (and view it as an opportunity rather than an obstacle), the better positioned you'll be to weather any storm.

Chapter 7: The Future's So Bright

CHAPTER 7 RESOURCES and IMPLEMENTATION TOOLS

Chapter 7: The Future's So Bright

Resources And Implementation Tools

To help you put these concepts into action, we've prepared several resources available at

OfficialOlsons.com/path

Essential Downloads:

✓ Success Metrics Dashboard

✓ Growth Planning Template

Bonus Materials:

- Long-term strategy guides
- Business valuation tool

Next Steps:

1. Set up your metrics dashboard
2. Create your growth plan
3. Define your long-term goals
4. Schedule quarterly reviews

Chapter 8: Pulling it All Together

P.A.T.H. - Prospect. Assess. Test. Harvest

Chapter 8: Pulling it All Together

Throughout this book, we've broken down the framework into its essential components, examining each piece of the puzzle that creates Amazon FBA success. Now it's time to see how these pieces fit together to create a complete, working system. Whether you're just starting your Amazon journey or looking to optimize your existing operation, this chapter will show you how to integrate each element of the framework into a cohesive, profitable business model that you can implement immediately and scale systematically over time. This can be a kind of operational blueprint - where theory meets practice, and knowledge transforms into action.

Understanding Your P.A.T.H.

Before we dive into implementation, let's review how each component of the framework builds upon the others to create a complete business system. These components are the gears in a well-oiled machine - each one must turn properly for the entire mechanism to function effectively.

The **Prospect Phase** focuses on finding VIABLE ASINs through systematic evaluation. Using the

Chapter 8: Pulling it All Together

Pre-Flight Inspection process, you identify listings that meet basic criteria for potential success. This isn't just about finding products - it's about building a pipeline of opportunities that can fuel your business growth. Every VIABLE ASIN you identify becomes a candidate for further evaluation, creating a steady stream of possibilities.

Moving into the **Assessment Phase**, you apply the **3-Step Check** to transform VIABLE ASINs into TESTABLE opportunities. This critical transition separates promising candidates from the merely possible. By evaluating velocity, capital protection, and profit potential, you identify products worth investing your time and money to test. This systematic approach removes the guesswork from your decision-making process.

The **Test Phase** converts these carefully selected candidates into REPLENISHABLE ASINs through a structured **4-Week Test** evaluation process. Rather than hoping for success, you gather concrete data about each product's performance in the real world. This methodical approach helps you make evidence-based decisions about which products deserve a permanent place in your inventory.

Finally, the **Harvest Phase** transforms successful tests into sustainable profit centers. Here, you optimize your winners, establish reliable reordering

P.A.T.H. - Prospect. Assess. Test. Harvest

systems, and implement the operational framework that allows your business to scale. This is where your Amazon business evolves from a collection of products into a predictable, sustainable, scalable operation.

These components work together in a continuous improvement cycle. Each successful REPLENISHABLE ASIN provides insights that improve your ability to identify future VIABLE ASINs. Every TESTABLE ASIN that does not become a REPLENISHABLE ASIN teaches valuable lessons about assessment criteria. The system becomes more refined and effective as you gain experience with each phase.

Common integration points emerge as you work through this cycle. Your VIABLE ASIN database feeds your testing pipeline. Test results inform your assessment criteria. Successful ASIN tests guide your prospecting efforts toward similar opportunities. Each component strengthens the others, creating a robust system that becomes more effective over time.

Think of it as a learning system that gets smarter with use. Every product you evaluate, test, and either add to your inventory or reject provides data that makes future decisions more accurate. This continuous improvement loop transforms your

Chapter 8: Pulling it All Together

Amazon business from a series of individual decisions into a systematic approach to building sustainable success.

Your First 90 Days and Beyond

Success in Amazon FBA comes from taking consistent, methodical action. Let's break down your implementation timeline into manageable phases that build upon each other, creating a clear roadmap for your first 90 days and beyond.

Your First 30 Days: Building the Foundation

Your initial few weeks focuses on establishing core systems and completing essential setup tasks. Start by opening your seller account with Amazon (this can sometimes take a couple of weeks). Install and familiarize yourself with key tools like Keepa and set up your basic tracking systems. Don't overcomplicate this - a simple spreadsheet or notebook can serve as your VIABLE ASIN database for now. Spend time practicing the **Pre-Flight Inspection** process on at least 80-100 listings until you can confidently evaluate products. By week two, you should be identifying your first potential test candidates. Use this time to bookmark your favorite sites, set up cash-back accounts and prepare for your first inventory orders. Remember,

P.A.T.H. - *Prospect. Assess. Test. Harvest*

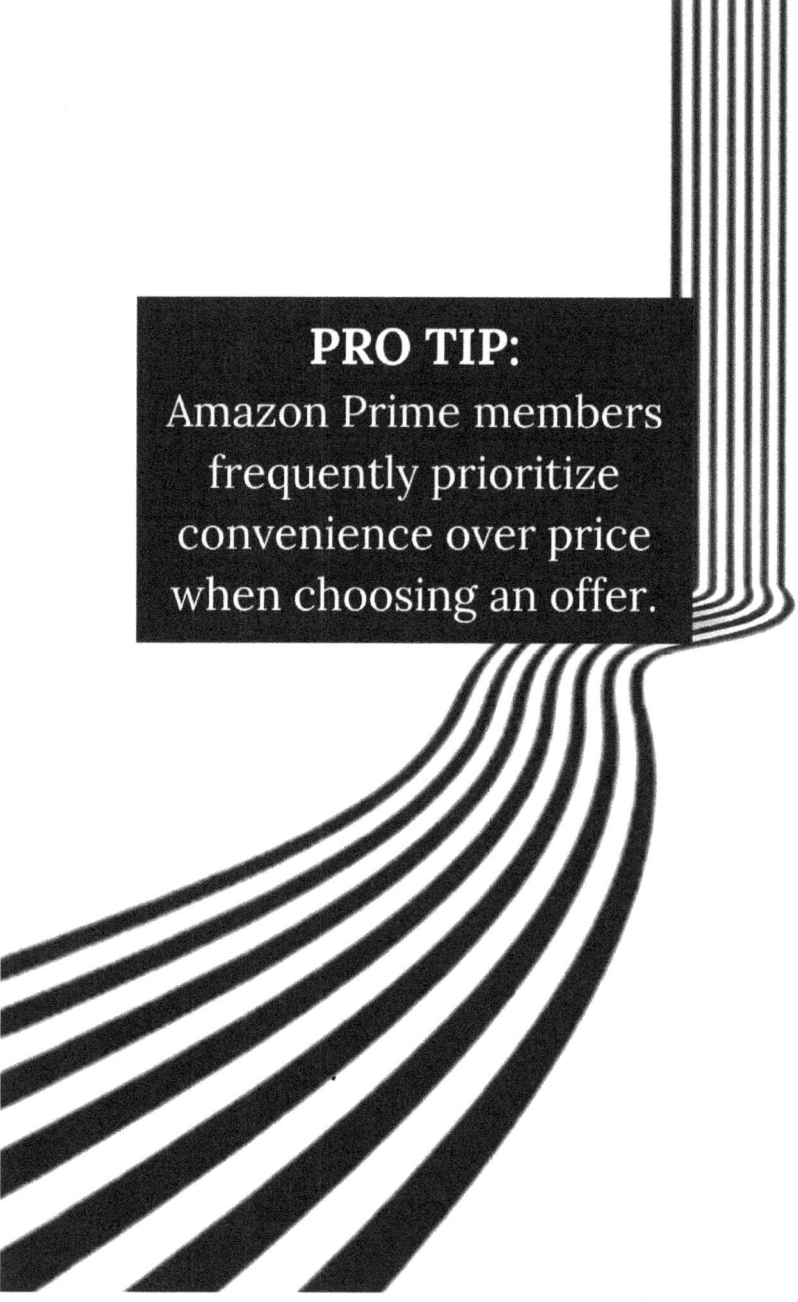

PRO TIP: Amazon Prime members frequently prioritize convenience over price when choosing an offer.

this phase is about practicing, learning and getting your systems set up, not rushing to make sales.

Days 31-90: Testing and Learning

This crucial period is where theory meets practice. Begin your first test cycles with small quantities (3-5 units) of carefully selected products. Run multiple tests simultaneously - aim to have a minimum of 5 test ASINs sent in each week. If you're going with the minimum of 5 as we teach, you will have about 20 ASINs in various stages of testing at any given time. Document your experience: pricing changes, customer feedback, delivery time impacts, and seasonal factors. This data becomes invaluable for future decision-making. By day 60, you could be identifying your first REPLENISHABLE ASINs and beginning to establish reorder patterns. Use this phase to refine your processes and build confidence in your decision-making abilities.

90+ Days: Scaling and Optimization

With your first successful tests complete and initial REPLENISHABLE ASINs identified, focus shifts to scaling and optimization. Begin building your product portfolio systematically, always maintaining a pipeline of new products to test while scaling successful ones. This is when you start seeing the compound effect of your earlier work -

P.A.T.H. - Prospect. Assess. Test. Harvest

using data from successful products to identify similar opportunities and optimizing your inventory management systems.

Your operational rhythm should now include:

- Weekly product sourcing sessions
- Systematic inventory reviews
- Monthly performance analysis
- Quarterly strategy adjustments

This period is also when you begin optimizing each aspect of your business:

- Refining your product selection criteria based on actual results
- Improving inventory turnover rates
- Enhancing profit margins through better sourcing strategies
- Developing more efficient operational systems

Remember, this timeline serves as a guide, not a rigid schedule. Some sellers progress faster; others take more time to build confidence. What matters is maintaining consistent forward momentum while building solid operational foundations. Your goal isn't speed - it's building a sustainable, scalable business that can grow with you over time.

Overcoming Common Challenges

Every Amazon seller faces obstacles on their path to success. Let's address the most common challenges and provide practical solutions that have helped hundreds of our program participants overcome these hurdles.

Breaking Through Analysis Paralysis

The most prevalent challenge new sellers face is analysis paralysis - the inability to move forward due to overthinking and over-analyzing. We've seen countless participants stuck in endless research loops, afraid to take action. The solution lies in our systematic approach: follow the **Pre-Flight Inspection** process, trust the **3-Step Check**, and start with small test quantities. Remember, you're not making a lifetime commitment to a product - you're conducting a controlled experiment with defined parameters and limited risk. Set specific deadlines for decision-making, and when in doubt, return to the fundamental question: Can you protect your capital while gathering real-world data?

P.A.T.H. - Prospect. Assess. Test. Harvest

Smart Capital Management

Managing your investment capital effectively requires balancing risk and opportunity. Start with small test quantities (3-5 units) across multiple products rather than going all-in on a single opportunity. Establish clear capital allocation rules: define your maximum investment per test, maintain a reserve for reordering proven winners, and never invest more than you can afford to have tied up for 60-90 days. Track your capital efficiency by measuring inventory turn rates and return on investment for each product. Most importantly, remember that protecting your capital takes priority over maximizing immediate profits.

Mastering Time Management

Success in Amazon FBA doesn't require 60-hour weeks, but it does demand consistent, focused effort. Create a structured schedule that allocates specific time blocks for key activities:

- Daily: 30-60 minutes for monitoring listings and basic maintenance

- Weekly: 8-15 hours for product research and ordering from suppliers and prepping & shipping your products (or in communications with your prep & ship service)

Chapter 8: Pulling it All Together

- Monthly: 2-4 hours for performance analysis and strategy adjustment

- Quarterly: 1 day for comprehensive business review and planning

Focus on high-impact activities during your peak energy hours. Use tools and templates to automate repetitive tasks. Remember, consistency trumps intensity - regular, systematic action builds sustainable success.

Navigating Scaling Challenges

As your business grows, new challenges emerge. Inventory management becomes more complex, capital requirements increase, and maintaining quality control across more products demands better systems. Address these challenges by:

- Developing standard operating procedures (SOPs) for routine tasks

- Creating systematic reordering processes

- Building relationships with multiple suppliers

- Implementing inventory management tools

- Establishing clear performance metrics

P.A.T.H. - Prospect. Assess. Test. Harvest

Most importantly, maintain the discipline that got you here - continue running **Pre-Flight Inspection**s and following the **3-Step Check** and the **4-Week Test**, even as your experience grows.

Avoiding Common Pitfalls

Learn from the mistakes we've seen repeatedly:

- Don't chase "perfect products" - focus on building a portfolio of solid performers

- Avoid emotional attachment to any single product

- Never compromise on supplier verification

- Don't neglect your VIABLE ASIN pipeline when things are going well

- Resist the urge to overcomplicate your systems

- Stay focused on your core metrics rather than getting distracted by endless data points

Remember, most serious setbacks in Amazon FBA come not as a result of what sellers are doing wrong, but because of departing from proven processes in search of shortcuts or "perfect" opportunities.

Chapter 8: Pulling it All Together

Success in Amazon FBA comes from consistent application of proven principles, not from finding secret shortcuts or "perfect products". By acknowledging these common challenges and implementing systematic solutions, you can build a resilient business capable of sustained growth.

Measuring and Optimizing Your Success

Understanding and tracking the right metrics transforms your Amazon business from a collection of products into a data-driven operation. Let's explore how to measure what matters and use that information to drive continuous improvement.

Essential Key Performance Indicators (KPIs)

Successful Amazon sellers focus on metrics that directly impact business health and growth. Your core KPIs should include:

Financial Metrics:

- Return on Investment (ROI) per ASIN
- Overall profit margins
- Inventory turn rates

Operational Metrics:

- Number of VIABLE ASINs identified weekly

P.A.T.H. - Prospect. Assess. Test. Harvest

- Test success rate
- Reorder accuracy
- Supplier reliability scores
- Account health rating

Growth Metrics:

- Number of REPLENISHABLE ASINs
- Monthly revenue trends
- Category diversification
- Seasonal performance patterns

Building Effective Tracking Systems

Your tracking system should be simple enough to maintain consistently but robust enough to provide actionable insights. Start with basic spreadsheets tracking:

- Product performance data
- Inventory levels and reorder points
- Supplier information and pricing
- Test results and learnings
- Capital allocation and returns

As your business grows, consider implementing more sophisticated tools, but remember - the best tracking system is the one you'll actually use consistently. Many successful sellers maintain surprisingly simple systems even as their businesses scale to six and seven figures.

Strategic Goal Setting and Adjustment

Set clear, measurable goals across three time frames:

Short-term (30 days):
- Number of new products to test
- Daily, weekly and monthly revenue targets
- Specific operational improvements

Medium-term (90 days):
- Portfolio expansion goals
- Profit margin improvements
- System optimization targets

Long-term (Annual):
- Revenue milestones
- Business model evolution
- Market position goals

Review and adjust these goals monthly, using actual performance data to refine your targets and strategies. Be willing to adjust goals based on market conditions and learning experiences but maintain commitment to your core business principles.

Continuous Performance Optimization

Use your metrics to drive ongoing improvement.

Weekly Reviews:

- Monitor inventory levels
- Track test progress
- Review sales patterns

Monthly Analysis:

- Evaluate product performance
- Assess capital efficiency
- Review goal progress
- Identify optimization opportunities

Quarterly Deep Dives:

- Comprehensive portfolio review
- Strategic planning updates

Chapter 8: Pulling it All Together

- System efficiency assessment
- Resource allocation review

Remember, the goal of tracking metrics isn't just to gather data - it's to inform better decisions and drive business improvement. Focus on metrics that guide action rather than those that simply provide information. Use your tracking systems to identify:

- Products ready for scaling
- ASINs needing optimization
- Opportunities for margin improvement
- Potential problem areas requiring attention

Success in Amazon FBA comes from making data-driven decisions while maintaining the flexibility to adapt to changing market conditions. Your metrics should serve as a dashboard guiding your business journey, not a straitjacket limiting your options.

Building Your Success Network

Successful Amazon sellers do not operate in isolation. Creating a strong support system accelerates your growth, helps you avoid common pitfalls, and provides valuable perspectives on your business journey. This network can be a kind of personal advisory board, combining tools, relationships, and knowledge resources.

P.A.T.H. - Prospect. Assess. Test. Harvest

Success leaves clues, and smart sellers take advantage of available resources. Beyond essential tools like Keepa and inventory management systems, successful sellers maintain a curated collection of templates, calculators, and standard operating procedures. These resources shouldn't overwhelm you - focus on tools that directly support your daily operations and decision-making processes rather than letting the tool dictate your business operations.

Amazon seller communities offer invaluable support through both online and in-person connections. Active participation yields better results than passive observation - share your experiences, ask questions, and contribute to discussions. These connections can lead to joint buying opportunities, shared market insights, and collaborative problem-solving. Remember, today's peer might become tomorrow's mentor or business partner.

Continuous education becomes crucial as the Amazon marketplace evolves. Rather than trying to learn everything at once, focus on knowledge that directly impacts your current business phase. Whether through formal training programs or informal peer learning, prioritize practical knowledge you can implement immediately. The most successful sellers typically spend 2-3 hours weekly on focused learning, often combining structured courses with real-world application.

Mentorship accelerates success by helping you learn from others' experiences. The best mentoring relationships are built on clear objectives, regular communication, and mutual respect. Look for mentors who have achieved what you're working toward but remember that valuable guidance can come from various sources - experienced sellers, business coaches, or even peers facing similar challenges.

Your success network should evolve as your business grows, continuously adding new resources and relationships while maintaining those that provide ongoing value. Think of it as a living system that requires regular nurturing but rewards you with compound returns on your investment of time and energy.

Maintaining Your Success Momentum

Building a successful Amazon FBA business isn't a sprint - it's a marathon that requires sustained effort and continuous adaptation. The key to long-term success lies not in occasional bursts of activity but in maintaining steady momentum through both challenges and victories.

P.A.T.H. - Prospect. Assess. Test. Harvest

We've said that consistency is key. We even made up a word for it: *ConsistenceKey*! However, because the frequency of your consistency also matters (being consistent once a quarter with the key aspects of your business is not frequently enough!), we created another new word: *ConfrequenceKey*.

We've been at this long enough to know that staying motivated requires more than initial enthusiasm. Create systems that generate their own momentum by celebrating small wins while keeping sight of larger goals. We would like to suggest that you track your progress visually, whether through a simple chart showing your growing number of REPLENISHABLE ASINs or a dashboard displaying increasing monthly revenues. These visible reminders of progress help maintain motivation during challenging periods. Remember, every successful seller faces moments of doubt - what separates the successful from the frustrated is their response to these moments.

The Amazon marketplace constantly evolves, making adaptability crucial for sustained success. Platform policies change, competition emerges, and consumer preferences shift. Rather than viewing these changes as obstacles, successful sellers treat them as opportunities to strengthen their businesses. Stay informed about marketplace trends, but don't let every change derail your core

Chapter 8: Pulling it All Together

strategy. Focus on building flexible systems that can adapt to changes while maintaining your fundamental business principles.

Continuous improvement comes from regular review and refinement of your operations. Schedule monthly performance reviews to identify areas for optimization. Look for patterns in your successful products to guide future sourcing decisions. Analyze failed tests for valuable lessons. Each experience, whether positive or negative, contains insights that can strengthen your business. The goal isn't perfection - it's consistent progress through iterative improvement.

Develop clear visions for your business at different scale levels. What systems need to be in place to handle double your current volume? Triple? What skills will you need to develop? What additional resources will become necessary? By anticipating future needs while managing current operations, you position your business for sustainable growth rather than reactive scaling.

Success in Amazon FBA comes from maintaining forward momentum while leveraging increasingly robust business systems. Think of it as building a flywheel - initial progress might be slow, but consistent effort creates momentum that makes future growth easier and more predictable.

EPILOGUE

P.A.T.H. - Prospect. Assess. Test. Harvest

EPILOGUE

Dawn breaks on an ordinary Friday, but this moment is anything but ordinary. Your hand trembles slightly as you reach for your phone, following your daily ritual of checking the Amazon seller app. Then you see it—the number that changes everything. Your first $1,000 day glows on the screen like a beacon of possibility, and suddenly you're wide awake, heart pounding with the realization: This is real. This is happening. This is yours.

In this quiet morning moment, time seems to stand still as the magnitude of your achievement sinks in. This isn't just a number, it's validation of every decision, every late night, every moment of doubt when you chose to push forward instead of giving up. Your journey flashes through your mind: the careful application of the framework, the meticulous identification of VIABLE ASINs, the thoughtful selection of TESTABLE opportunities, and the patient nurturing of REPLENISHABLE products. Each step, each decision, each small victory led you here.

A warm sense of pride wells up as you realize this business you've built is more than a side hustle—it's a testament to your courage, persistence, and

Epilogue

vision. Whether this success means freedom from debt, the ability to quit your day job, or the first step toward building generational wealth, you've proven something powerful to yourself: you can do this. You are doing this!

Your mind races forward through the possibilities that now seem within reach—$2,000 days, $10,000 weeks, six-figure months. But something deeper stirs within you: the recognition that these metrics, while important, are just markers on a greater journey. This is about building something lasting, something that grows beyond you, something that creates value for others while creating freedom for yourself.

Yet even as you celebrate this milestone, you feel a familiar spark of excitement about what comes next. Because you've learned something crucial on this journey: success isn't a destination, it's a series of elevating achievements, each one opening doors to new possibilities you couldn't see before. It's not just a trite saying anymore...it actually applies to you.

This moment, your first $1,000 day, isn't the end of your story, it's a powerful beginning. You've built more than a revenue stream; you've developed skills, judgment, and confidence that will serve you through every future challenge and opportunity.

P.A.T.H. - Prospect. Assess. Test. Harvest

You've proven you can learn, adapt, and overcome. Most importantly, you've shown yourself that with the right framework and persistent effort, remarkable achievements are within your grasp.

Take a moment to let this sink in. Celebrate this victory. You've earned it. But know that this is just one milestone on your path to even greater accomplishments. The journey ahead is filled with possibilities you're now ready to explore.

Remember to stay connected with your community of fellow sellers, continue learning and growing, and keep pushing the boundaries of what you believe is possible. Your success story is still being written, and its potential is limited only by your imagination and determination.

This is your moment. This is your path. And we couldn't be more excited to see where it leads you next.

Here's to your journey—past, present, and the brilliant future you're building.

All our best!
Brian & Robin Joy

INDEX

3-Step Check 5, 66, 71, 74–75, 77, 94, 105–106, 112, 181, 187, 190

4-Week Test 5, 109, 112, 115, 117, 124, 132, 137, 139, 181, 190

A

Amazon FBA ix, 3–4, 7–8, 12, 15–16, 21, 26–27, 34, 47, 50, 53, 56, 69, 82, 106, 137, 167, 180, 183, 188, 190–191, 195, 197, 199

Assessment Phase 5, 68, 74, 143, 181

B

Break-Even Price 84–85, 94, 130, 136

Bridging the Gap 4, 49, 58, 74

C

Capital Protection 77, 83–84, 94, 113, 181

Confrequencekey 198

Consistencekey 198

F

Framework 7, v, vii, x, 3–4, 7, 21, 69, 82, 94, 105–106, 115, 170, 180, 182, 202, 204

H

Harvest Phase 5, 142–143, 181

K

Keepa x–xi, 24–29, 31, 82–84, 104, 109, 116, 119–120, 183, 196

P

P.A.T.H. 7, v, vii, x, 3–4, 7, 21, 69, 180

Pre-Flight Inspection 4, 35, 46, 69, 74, 112, 181, 183, 187, 190

Profit Potential 35, 77, 83, 90, 94, 113, 157, 181

Prospect Phase 4, 34, 63, 68, 180

R

REPLENISHABLE ASIN 5, 91, 101, 106, 112, 114, 128–129, 137, 142, 144, 154, 157, 162, 171, 181–182, 185, 192, 198

T

Test Phase 5, 112, 181

TESTABLE ASIN 5, 74, 77, 101, 106, 142, 150, 158, 162, 182

V

Velocity 26, 64, 77, 79, 83, 94, 144, 154, 181

VIABLE ASIN 4, 63, 68–69, 71, 74, 105, 112, 129, 142, 162, 180–183, 190–191, 202

www.ingramcontent.com/pod-product-compliance
Lightning Source LLC
Chambersburg PA
CBHW032053090426
42744CB00005B/201